Wood Carving and Whittling for Everyone

Other books by the author

Simple Colonial Furniture
How to Design Period Furniture
Design for the Craftsman
You Can Whittle and Carve (with Amanda W. Hellum)
Making Useful Things of Wood
Heirloom Furniture
Wood Carving and Whittling Made Easy
Furniture of Pine, Poplar and Maple
How to Make Colonial Furniture
Reproducing Antique Furniture

FRANKLIN H. GOTTSHALL

Wood Carving and Whittling for Everyone

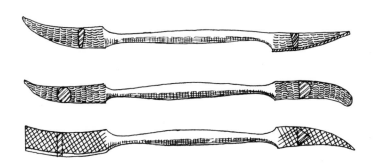

Charles Scribner's Sons   NEW YORK

Copyright © 1977 Franklin H. Gottshall

Library of Congress Cataloging in Publication Data

Gottshall, Franklin H
    Wood carving and whittling for everyone.

    Includes index.
    1. Wood-carving—Technique. I. Title.
TT199.7.G66   736'.4   77-23224
ISBN 0-684-14886-2

1 3 5 7 9 11 13 15 17 19 MD/C 20 18 16 14 12 10 8 6 4 2

Printed in the United States of America

Selections used with the permission of Crown Publishers, Inc., from REPRODUCING ANTIQUE FURNITURE by Franklin H. Gottshall, copyright © 1971 by Franklin H. Gottshall.

Selections redrawn with the permission of Macmillan Publishing Co., Inc., from WOODCARVING AND WHITTLING MADE EASY by Franklin H. Gottshall, copyright © 1963 Franklin H. Gottshall.

Selections are reprinted from DESIGN FOR THE CRAFTSMAN by Franklin H. Gottshall, copyright 1940 Franklin H. Gottshall and from CRAFTWORK IN METAL, WOOD, LEATHER, PLASTICS by Franklin H. Gottshall, copyright 1954 Franklin H. Gottshall.

The line drawing of the Christmas Elf is the original work of Norman E. Hosie, of Lexington, Kentucky, and is used with his permission.

Other selections are used with the permission of Leon M. Reinert, Frank Updegrove, and Mrs. Jack P. Hellum.

Acknowledgments

I AM grateful to many people for their help in preparing this book:

Mr. Frank Updegrove, a wood-carver in Boyertown, Pennsylvania, who allowed me to photograph and make working drawings of ten of his animal projects. Mr. Updegrove started carving animals years ago when he worked with the Barnum and Bailey Circus and is still an active carver. At one time he carved an entire circus, which unfortunately was later lost in a fire. I am proud to include a sampling of his work in Projects 21 through 29.

Mr. Norman E. Hosie of Lexington, Kentucky, for permission to use the Christmas elves he designed and carved, and for the drawings and photographs of his work seen in Project 31.

Mr. Leon Reinert of Boyertown, who gave me permission to make drawings of the Indian carving described in Project 32 and to photograph it

for use in this book. The carving was designed and executed by his friend the late Frederich Herricht, a talented wood-carver who served his apprenticeship in Germany.

A good friend who wishes to remain anonymous, for permission to include the cutting board in Project 1, which is a part of his collection of antiques.

My son, Bruce H. Gottshall, who did most of the photographs for the book.

The editors of *Popular Science* for permission to use material I provided for a book they published and which I have revised and adapted for use in several projects in this book.

Mr. Edward F. Gallenstein, president of the National Wood Carvers' Association and editor of the association's bimonthly magazine, *Chip Chats*, for his enthusiastic promotion of the association and for his interest in its members' activities.

To Agnes, my wife, whose encouragement, suggestions, and counseling are invaluable

Contents

Preface

THE fact that new books on the art of wood carving are appearing with ever greater frequency comes as no great surprise to those of us who enjoy this fascinating and engrossing hobby. The National Wood Carvers' Association boasts over ten thousand members, most of whom are amateurs pursuing their hobby for the pleasure they get out of it. Wood-carving shows and conventions are attracting larger and larger crowds.

Most books on wood carving are limited in subject matter to purely decorative objects. I feel, however, that a work of art can sometimes serve a useful function in the home, and so I have included projects with both aesthetic and practical appeal.

I have also made an effort to give as much practical information as possible to the amateur and to the more experienced carver by providing comprehensive working drawings and photographs of each project.

1

Tools and Equipment

A GOOD pocketknife and the means for sharpening it are the only prerequisites for beginning to carve.

My first bit of carving was a chip-carved star on a piece of scrap pine. done with a pocketknife. I was so pleased with my first venture into this phase of woodworking that I decided to try a much more ambitious piece, the chip-carved box shown in Project 4. All the carving on this box was done with a knife; the outlining for the grooves was chiseled into the lid for the inlay banding.

Much wood carving can be done with very few tools. I have seen lavishly equipped workshops from which very little good work was produced and, conversely, have been amazed by work of exceptional quality produced in shops with seemingly inadequate equipment. The difference is in the training, ability, and resourcefulness of the craftsman who does the work. In the hands of a reasonably able craftsman much can be done with little.

Of course, I do not mean to give the impression that quality equipment is of no consequence. I urge you to acquire good tools and adequate facilities if you put them to good use. In this book I concentrate on basic tools but give suggestions for more elaborate equipment for those who are interested.

Wood-carvers usually start with whittling, a form of carving in which a knife is the only tool used. With a sharp tool, some planning, and a minimum of instruction, the greenest novice should be able to produce a recognizable object like the small elephant being whittled in Figure 1.

Figure 1. With a sharp tool, some planning, and a minimum of instruction, the greenest novice can produce a recognizable object.

Knives

While there are knives of many types and sizes and a wide variety of blades, I have found that for all practical purposes very few different types of blades are actually needed. Figure 2 shows several of the more common types. While an advanced whittler may prefer a greater variety of shapes, they are not a requirement.

The spear point, if the blade is large or even medium size, is suitable for rough cutting and rounding sharp edges when beginning a carving. The clip blade is an all-purpose blade; its shape adapts to outlining around a pattern drawn on the wood, to trimming, to slicing; and if the end is sharpened to a fine point, it will do fine detail work such as cutting and forming an eye. However, thin, lighter blades like the pen blade are

2

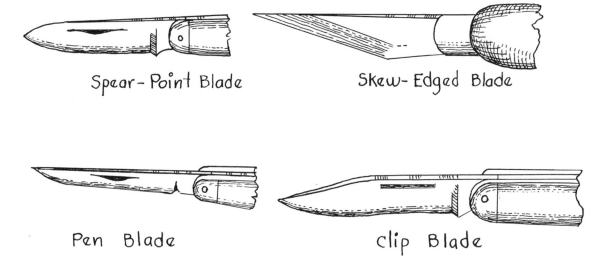

Spear-Point Blade   Skew-Edged Blade

Pen Blade   clip Blade

Figure 2. Four common knife blades.

usually better for this purpose. Figure 5 shows how the blade is held to start carving an eye.

The skew blade is best for doing chip carving with a knife and was the kind used to do the box in Project 4. The point is suitable for outlining the design and for driving the initial incising cuts deep enough so that the following slicing cuts can easily remove the wood.

Figure 3 shows two knives with fixed blades: A is a skew-bladed knife, and B is a clip-bladed knife, often referred to as a sloyd knife. When the blade is fixed in its handle, it will not accidentally fold under the pressure of cutting, a welcome safety feature.

It is very important, of course, to keep knife blades sharp and the bevel or cutting edge prop-

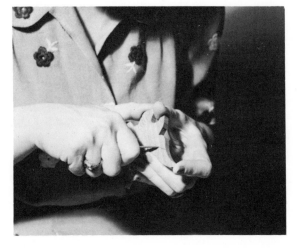

TOP *Figure 3.* Two knives with fixed blades: skew blade (left), and clip blade (right).

ABOVE *Figure 4.* Four types of folding blades.

RIGHT *Figure 5.* Holding a pen blade to start carving an eye.

erly formed; instructions for doing so are given later in this chapter.

While it is entirely feasible to whittle a small animal using nothing more than a knife, the work is made considerably easier if the block of wood is first sawed to an approximate shape—if possible with an electrically powered band saw or jigsaw, or by hand with an inexpensive coping saw. Once the blank has been sawed to shape, the actual carving consists of little more than just rounding off the roughly squared corners. Further refining and smoothing can be done with fine sandpaper, folded into a strip and rubbed back and forth over the piece.

Chisels

Another tool that makes the whittler's job easier is the carver's chisel, which can be used to trim and shape areas of work that are difficult to reach with a knife. The blade is held with the

thumb to keep it from going too far or too fast, and the fingers holding the work in front of the chisel should be kept well below the cutting edge (Figure 6).

While a knife is a versatile tool and an excellent one for the beginner to start with, all professionals and most amateurs find that a set of good carving chisels and some additional tools will add immeasurably to the scope and variety of the work they can do. Such a set of tools need not be large, especially if you are just starting to carve, but should be of the highest quality obtainable. Carving chisels made in England and Germany have a reputation for quality, and excellent tools are sold by American firms. I do not recommend buying a prepackaged set of tools because the shapes usually found in such sets seldom allow enough flexibility for a beginner's needs. I suggest selecting the tools a few at a time. A good beginning set might include the following:

two No. 1 straight chisels, ⅛″ and ¼″ width
one No. 2 skew chisel, ⅜″ width
one No. 4 extra-flat, ½″ width
one No. 6 gouge, 3/16″ width
one No. 5 gouge, ⅜″ width
one No. 11 gouge, ½″ width
one No. 11 veiner, ⅛″ width
one No. 11 fluter, ¼″ width
one No. 5 gouge, ⅛″ width
one No. 42 long-bent V-tool, ⅜″
one No. 43 or No. 44 short-bent V-tool

Some of these chisels are shown in Figure 7.

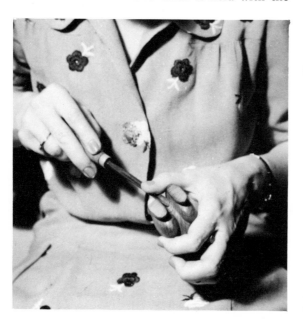

Figure 6. Using a carver's chisel to trim parts difficult to reach with a knife.

Photo courtesy Buck Bros. Tool Co.

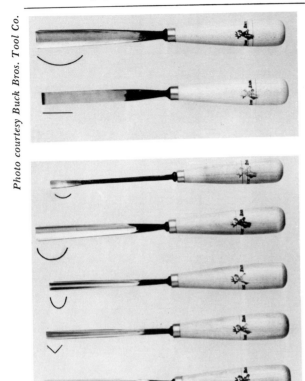

Figure 8 shows a number of my own tools. Among these are two not mentioned in the beginner's list but which I have found extremely useful. They are the two tools on the extreme left, known as a macaroni shape, or square-U. This tool is excellent for working and trimming outlines where sharp, square shoulders are to be formed. It is also useful for shaping curved areas. I recommend one ¼″ wide as first choice; two sizes are shown in Figure 8: ¼″ and ⅜″.

On the extreme right in Figure 8 are two dentist's chisels. The cutting edge on one of these is beveled on the bottom, and on the other one it is beveled on the upper side. The cutting edges are only 1⁄16″ wide, and both their shape and their size make them ideally suited for trimming wood in very small areas and tight corners.

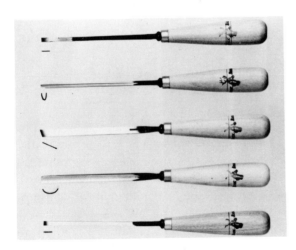

Figure 7. Twelve types of chisels.

Figure 8. A number of my own tools, including (on the left) a macaroni shape, or square-U chisel; and on the right, two dentist's chisels.

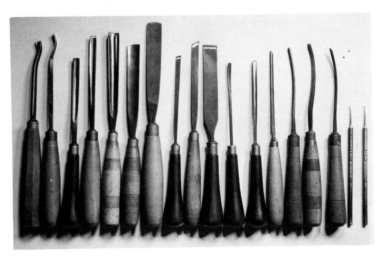

SWEEPS $\frac{1"}{16}$ TO $1\frac{1"}{2}$	NO.	NAME	LONG BENT	SPOON	BACK BENT	V-TOOLS
—	1	CHISELS		21		39 –WIDE
/	2	SKEW		22–23		40–MEDIUM
—	3	EXTRA-FLAT	12	24	33	41–NARROW
—	4	EXTRA-FLAT	13	25	34	42– LONG-BENT
—	5	GOUGES	14	26	35	43-SHORT-BENT
—	6	GOUGES	15	27	36	
◡	7	GOUGES	16	28	37	
◡	8	GOUGES	17	29	38	
◡	9	GOUGES	18	30		
◡	10	DEEP GOUGE	19	31		
◡	11	DEEP GOUGE	20	32		
◡	11	FLUTER				
V	11	VEINER				

Figure 9. Table of standardized kinds, sweeps, and sizes of carving chisels.

Good-quality carving chisels are numbered, and the numbers are standardized. Figure 9 shows a table with various kinds, sweeps, and sizes of carving chisels. The sweep refers to the curvature of the cutting edge of a gouge regardless of its width. Thus a No. 9 gouge on which the cutting edge approximates a semicircle would have this sweep in the narrower as well as the wider widths.

Figure 10 shows examples of each kind of chisel. Some have straight blades; others have long, gently curved blades (C and H in Figure 10). Some have a more pronounced, sharper bend, being almost spoon-shaped (I and M), and there are also back-bent tools (J)—a useful shape, incidentally, for forming toes on the ball-and-claw feet of Chippendale furniture.

Straight Chisels

Blades on wood-carving chisels are rather slender, and their cutting edges are ground differently from those usually found on ordinary woodworker's chisels. The straight chisel, instead of being beveled on only one side of the blade, is often beveled on both (Figure 10A). Others are ground on the skew (Figure 10B) to give a slicing cut as they are pushed through the wood. This shape is particularly effective for smooth cutting

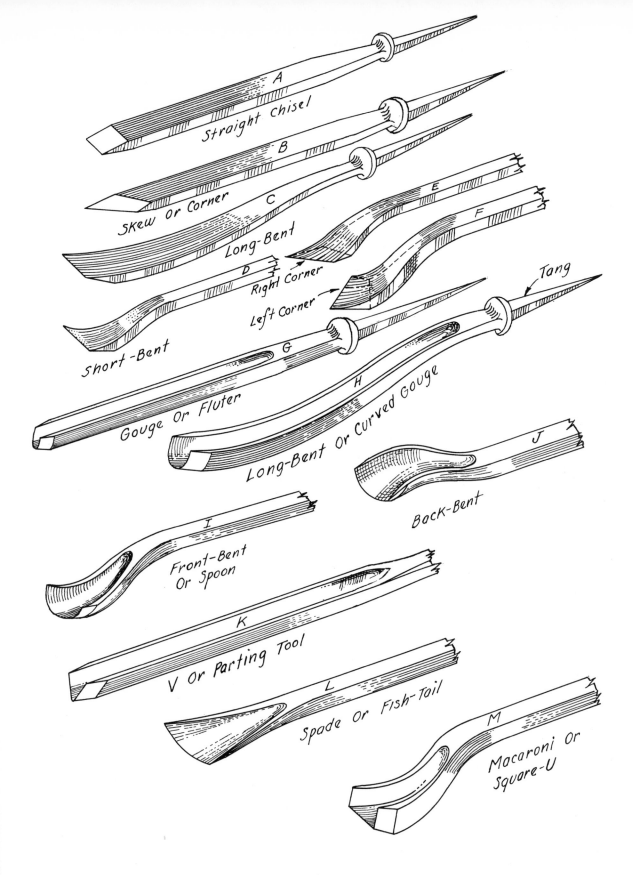

A — Straight Chisel

B — Skew Or Corner

C — Long-Bent

D — Short-Bent

E — Right Corner

F — Left Corner

G — Gouge Or Fluter

H — Long-Bent Or Curved Gouge

Tang

I — Front-Bent Or Spoon

J — Back-Bent

K — V Or Parting Tool

L — Spade Or Fish-Tail

M — Macaroni Or Square-U

Figure 10. Examples of each kind of chisel.

7

across the grain. Straight chisels are used for cutting or trimming straight lines and edges and for trimming and truing up corners; when hammered with a mallet, they can be driven deep into the wood. This makes them the primary tools for the heavy cutting necessary to form the outlines of a design, as shown in Figure 11, so that the background surrounding the design can be removed later. When used for trimming, truing up, and smoothing, they are often firmly held by the blade with one hand and pushed through the wood with the other, as shown in Figure 12.

Where heavy roughing out of waste is necessary, the more sturdy socket-firmer carpenter's chisel, or gouge, may be used as shown in Figure 13. Here we also use the hammer-type mallet. Later on, when most of the waste material has been chopped out, the finer wood-carving chisels are used to smooth up and finish the work.

Figure 11. Using a straight chisel with a mallet to form the outlines of a design.

Figure 12. Using a chisel for trimming.

Figure 13. Using a socket-firmer carpenter's chisel, or gouge, with a hammer-type mallet for roughing-out.

Gouges

As seen on the table in Figure 9, gouge blades come in various curvatures, beginning with No. 3, called an extra-flat, a useful shape to use in smoothing backgrounds and for trimming edges of curves having a large radius. The more sharply curved gouges are used to cut deep grooves. Gouges with straight shafts are the most frequently used, being the workhorses of the carver's kit. Curved gouges and spoons are used to remove wood where the curvature of the object prevents the use of a straight-bladed tool.

Short-Bent Tools

For cutting or trimming areas confined in close places, and especially those on which some undercutting is required, no other tool is so well adapted as the short-bent chisel or gouge. It can get to places not accessible to tools with straight or even the more gently curved blades. Figure 10D shows a short-bent chisel sharpened straight across, while E and F show tools on which the cutting edges are ground to an angle to get into corners sharper than a right angle. In addition to short-bent straight chisels and gouges I recommend the short-bent square-U-shaped tool already mentioned (Figure 10M). For some unexplained reason these are seldom listed or shown in carving tool catalogs. (Mine had to be specially

ordered and made for me.) I find they work better for trimming and squaring up outlines and making square shoulders than either the straight chisel or the V-tool. They are also good tools to use for truing up where a convex curve makes a sharp line meeting a flat surface.

Parting or V-tools

V-shaped tools, also known as parting tools, are among the most useful and versatile shapes in the wood-carver's kit. The tool I use most often when outlining a design is a No. 43 short-bent V-tool. The cutting edges of this tool are not more than $3/16''$ wide, and the shaft of the blade above the V is quite slender. The V is not curved as sharply as some of the other short-bent V-tools in my kit, but it is curved just enough to make it ideal for outlining a design. Since I have not run across another shaped just like it, I hone the cutting edges carefully to preserve the steel. V-tools come with straight, long-bent, and short-bent blades, and the V may be wide (almost a right angle), medium, or narrow. They are used to outline a design, make deep V-cuts, and trim outlines.

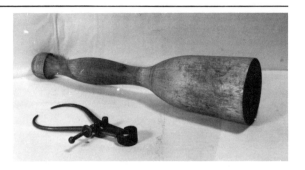

Spade Tools

Spade tools, like the one shown in Figure 10L, are used primarily for trimming, smoothing, and light cutting. They are seldom hammered with a mallet but are instead usually held by the blade with one hand and pushed or nudged along with the palm of the other hand.

Other Useful Tools

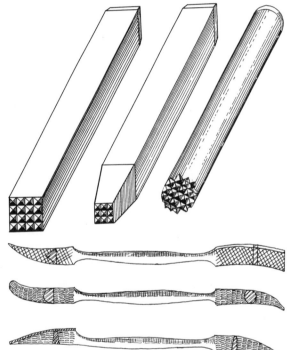

TOP *Figure 14.* Calipers (left) and wooden mallet (right).

CENTER *Figure 15A.* Carver's background punches.

BELOW *Figure 15B.* Carver's wood rasps.

If chisels are used, the wooden mallet is essential. While an ordinary hammer-type mallet is sometimes used for very heavy cutting (Figure 13), better shaped and better adapted to this specialized form of woodworking is the mallet shown in Figure 14. There are two advantages of this type of mallet over the hammer type: (1) you can use it without regard to how the handle is held and be sure it will hit the chisel handle a proper blow, and (2) the force of the blow and its direction are more easily controlled since you don't have to watch where the blow will land.

The calipers, also shown in Figure 14, are a very useful measuring tool for determining thicknesses at various points of a carving. A 1′ straight-edged ruler is also required.

Carver's background punches (Figure 15A), though not often needed, can be useful occasionally. The same is true of wood files and rasps. Truly accomplished craftsmen seldom use punches and try to avoid filing their carvings if they can be properly finished otherwise. While sanding is necessary in more cases than not, even this should be held to a minimum. There are, however, times and places where punches may be used to improve the work or give it surface texture of a kind no knife or chisel can imitate. The background of the design for the wastebasket in Project 2 is well adapted to this type of treatment.

Rasps like the small ones shown in Figure 15B and even larger wood files are sometimes the only tools you can use to smooth certain areas of a wood carving. The files should be used before the final sanding. I prefer metal rasps to ordinary wood files because they have narrower ends and will therefore fit into smaller openings. Some filing was done on the outside of the fruit bowl in Project 19 when the chiseling had been completed.

As can be seen in many of the photographs in this book, a good woodworker's vise, C-clamps, and sometimes wooden hand screws are used to hold work while it is being carved.

Most woodworking benches are less than 36″ high, so low a height that using one for carving can be hard on your back. One way to solve this problem is to place two thick planks under the work and hold all this in place with C-clamps (Figure 31). By varying the number of planks you can determine the most comfortable height for you. This improvisation works well and helps prove my point that fancy special equipment is not necessary to do wood carving. However, for those who would prefer something better, Figure 16 shows a good carver's bench not too difficult or expensive for most workers to build. If bought ready-made it might cost several hundred dollars, but it can be built in a home workshop very inexpensively.

Sharpening Tools

Wood-carving tools should be kept properly ground and honed at all times. Both knives and chisels should be carefully ground, but once cutting edges are ground on a wheel to the proper bevel—the angle formed where the edges meet—grinding should be held to a minimum, in order not to waste valuable metal and to ensure the long life of tools which can be quite expensive to replace. It is better to keep the tool sharp and in good working order on a fine-grit oilstone and with carver's slips than to let it get so dull or out of shape that frequent grinding is necessary. A motor-driven power grinder like the one shown in Figure 17 is best because it leaves both hands free to hold the tool. However, the cheaper hand-powered grinder shown in Figure 18 will also do. To use it you need another to turn the crank. Notice that the grinding wheel is rotated against the edge of the tool and not away from it.

I use a manufactured vitrified grinding wheel made of finely granulated aluminum oxide. The aluminum oxide wheel does not heat the tool as rapidly as a carborundum wheel would, and it self-cleans its surface better. The wheel can be used on the lathe, as shown in Figure 19. When chisels are ground it is best also to use the lathe tool rest to support the tool. This will make it easier to keep a light pressure on the wheel and prevent overheating of the tool. Dipping the tool in water frequently is a further safeguard.

The cutting edge should be ground to a narrow V-shape. Better yet, this V-shaped bevel should be slightly concave, which, if the tool is properly manipulated on the revolving wheel, will be the natural result of the grinding process since the grinding surface of the wheel is convex.

Grinding is the first step in putting a really keen edge on a tool. Once the tool has been ground to its proper bevel, it should be whetted and honed on a fine-grit oilstone. Both processes mean sharpening by hand on a stone; honing implies working the tool to a keener edge than just whetting. Keep oilstones wet with a mixture of equal parts of kerosene and light nondetergent machine oil. This prevents the stone from taking on a glazed surface from the ground-off metal particles. Figure 20 shows a knife being whetted

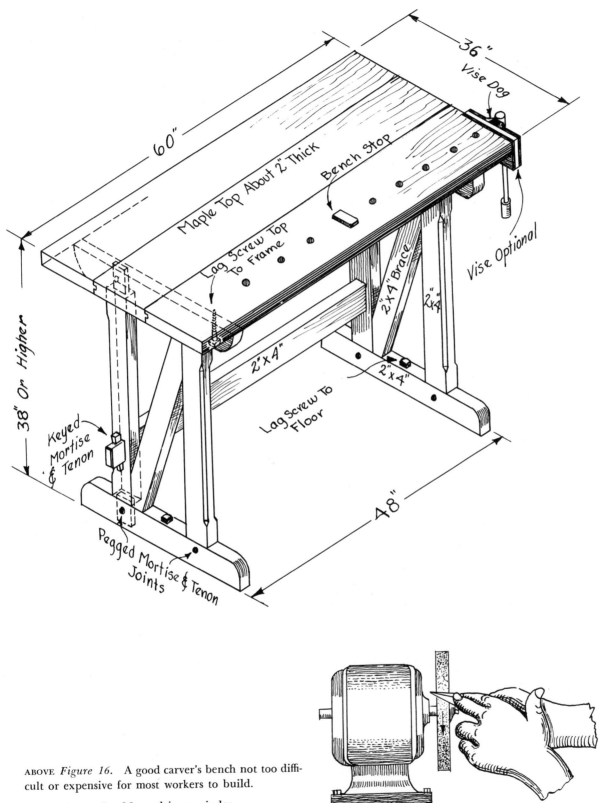

60"

36"

Vise Dog

Maple Top About 2" Thick

Bench Stop

Lag Screw Top To Frame

2"x4" Brace

2"x4"

Vise Optional

38" Or Higher

2"x4"

Lag Screw To Floor

2"x4"

Keyed Mortise & Tenon

Pegged Mortise & Tenon Joints

48"

ABOVE *Figure 16.* A good carver's bench not too difficult or expensive for most workers to build.

RIGHT *Figure 17.* Motor-driven grinder.

13

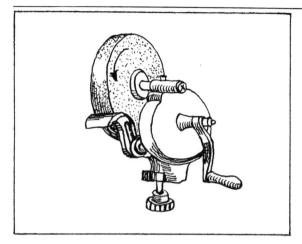

Direction of Rotation

TOP LEFT *Figure 18.* Hand-power grinder.

ABOVE *Figure 19.* Using vitrified grinding wheel on a lathe.

TOP RIGHT *Figure 20.* Whetting a knife on oilstone.

on the oilstone, and also the proper angle at which it should be held. Chisels and gouges are sharpened on the stone as shown in Figure 21C. Flat chisels are rotated while they are being whetted in the direction shown in Figure 21C. They are then turned over, laid flat upon the surface of the stone, and rubbed sideways across the stone to get rid of the wire edge. The wire edge is metal turned toward the flat side as the bevel is being rubbed over the stone. As soon as this appears on the flat side, the edge has been whetted sufficiently on that side. On gouges the wire edge must be removed with the rounded edge of a small slipstone, like the one shown in Figure 22A for wide chisels, or the smaller ones shown in Figure 22D and E for those that are narrower. Figure 22 shows oilstones and slips of various sizes and shapes. The piece of leather is used for stropping chisels after whetting them (Figure 22C).

The V-tool is probably the most difficult to sharpen, and of these the short-bent tools are the most troublesome. The reason for this is that you must be careful to sharpen the angle at the bottom as much as you do the sides or the chisel will not make clean cuts, especially across the grain of the wood. If properly sharpened, the V-tool will cut as crisply and cleanly across the grain as with it. The metal is thicker at the place where the two sides meet, and when sharpening the two

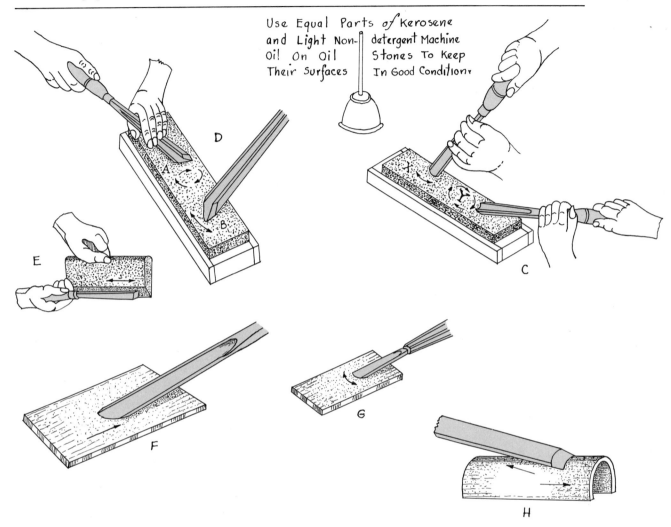

Use Equal Parts of Kerosene and Light Non-detergent Machine Oil On Oil Stones To Keep Their Surfaces In Good Condition.

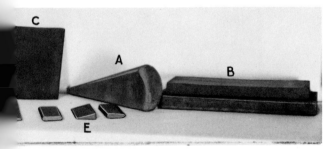

TOP *Figure 21.* Sharpening chisels or gouges on oilstone (C); rubbing chisel over stone (D); removing wire edge from inside of V-tool (E); stropping tools on pieces of leather (F, G, H).

ABOVE *Figure 22.* Slipstones for chisels of various widths.

sides the cutting edge at the angle has a tendency to be left protruding over the sides. To correct this, rub the chisel over the stone as shown in Figure 21D at B, until the protruding end is removed. V-tools also cut better if the bottom of the V is sloped back toward the handle of the tool, rather than grinding it at right angles to the baseline of the blade. The method for removing the wire edge from the inside of a V-tool is shown in Figure 21E.

After grinding, whetting, and honing the tools, you may strop them on pieces of leather dressed with fine emery paste or jeweler's rouge, or valve grinding compound with an oil base. This may be purchased at any auto supply store. The ways to do this are shown in Figures 21F, G, and H.

Glue

For the projects in this book water-soluble white glue is perfectly adequate. If necessary, it can be thinned with water. It will dry clear, and it is easy to use straight from the container. Elmer's is one of the best-known white glues.

A glance at the projects in this book will show that they involve several processes other than wood carving—joinery, cabinetmaking, even metalwork—but I have limited the instructions on these processes to only those necessary for the project at hand, as there are already many excellent books that deal extensively with each of these crafts.

2

Techniques
and Methods

ONE great advantage of whittling with a knife is that small objects can be held in one hand while the cutting is done with the other (Figure 23). Sometimes it is possible to hold the object in a vise to do some of the work (Figure 24) or to hold it against the table surface with clamps, as in Figure 25. The fact that the object can be held in the hand makes it easy to move it around and cut in almost any direction. And, of course, most whittling with a knife can be done while resting comfortably in a chair, a bonus not to be overlooked!

Large carvings, or those done on large planks or boards, must be held in a vise or with clamps. Because turning them frequently is inconvenient, cutting from one position is done as much as possible. As you do more and more carving, it pays to practice cutting from one position in all directions with a chisel. This skill saves time and is useful for working on larger objects that cannot be put in the vise in certain positions.

The greater part of the carving done on the animals shown in Chapter 4 was done with knives. A pattern showing the outline of the animal was first drawn on a piece of paper or cardboard (such a pattern is shown in Figure 24). After the wood has been selected, this outline is then transferred to one side of a blank. This is then sawed to shape on a band saw, or by hand with a coping saw. Figure 26 shows a blank sawed to shape to begin carving a bison. A center line is drawn around the top and bottom of the blank. Other lines can be added, indicating the position of tail, head, legs, and ears. As many more details as feasible should also be shown on the blank at this time. From time to time the carving process may remove lines which must be redrawn as work proceeds.

TOP LEFT *Figure 23*. Small objects can be held in your hand.

TOP RIGHT *Figure 24*. Whittling an object held by a vise. Note the cardboard pattern on the table.

LEFT *Figure 25*. Whittling an object held by clamps.

In Figure 27 the bison is shown partly carved. The general shape and thickness of various parts are relatively well established at this stage, and holes for the horns have been drilled. Waste, removed from around and between the legs, has been cut out with a coping saw with the body held in a vise. Most of the waste separating the tail from the body was removed with drills on a drill press.

Since the bison is quite large in relation to most whittlings, much of the preliminary rough cutting, or boasting-in as it is sometimes called, was done with shallow gouges, as was some of the shaping around the hips, back, and neck. Final trimming, smoothing, and shaping can then be done mostly with knives.

18

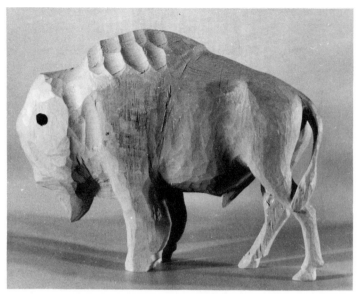

Figure 26. A blank sawed to shape to begin carving a bison.

Figure 27. Partly carved bison.

Once the body, head, legs, and other large areas have been properly shaped, all that remains to be done is to carve the more refined details, like eyes, ears, grooves simulating fur on the forelegs, and so on. The drawings and photographs for Project 23 show how this is done.

Scratch Carving, Incising, and Other Elementary Tool Techniques

Possibly the simplest and most elementary type of carving, sometimes referred to as scratch carving, consists of little more than lines cut into the wood with either a V-tool or a narrow veiner. A little of this is shown in the decorative carving near the lettering in Project 15. There's more of it with slightly deeper modeling on the back of the cutting board in Project 1. The Roman lettering of the quotation is carving of a similar type, done almost entirely with a short-bent V-tool.

Figure 28 shows a small board filled with patterns, which serves as a sampler of simple tool techniques. Carved on a small piece of kiln-dried yellow poplar, it illustrates the wide scope of decorative possibilities that can be achieved with various tools. I pass on to you the observation of a widely traveled fellow craftsman who told me he'd never met a bored wood-carver!

The exercise board shows lines cut with the V-tool and veiner. Shallow grooves are cut with a gouge between the V-grooves at 1, while at 3 the ridges between the V-grooves are rounded over with a skew chisel. Simulated rope carving is shown at 4, and 5 shows the steps in carving beads. These are formed by first making V-cuts almost perpendicular to the surface at the four corners of each bead and then trimming around these with narrow chisels and semicircular gouges. The patterns at 2 are made by hammer-

Figure 28. Sampler of simple tool techniques.

Figure 29. An example of flat-surface carving.

cut, but instead first to make a fairly light incision, and then with a skew knife or skew chisel slice to the incision. Once the outline has been established, successive repeats of these incisions and more slicing cuts will create the pattern.

ing a gouge straight down into the wood and then chiseling to it with the same gouge held at about a 45-degree angle. At 7 is shown an interesting background surface texture achieved with a gouge used on several carvings in this book. At 10 the carving simulates a basket weave, started with chisel cuts straight down into the wood and finished off with a short-bent V-tool and a skew chisel. The fish scales at 11 are done by cutting straight down with a No. 8 gouge and then trimming to it with shallow gouges. At 13 is shown the basic cut for all chip-carved designs. The perpendicular cuts should be made first by hammering a straight chisel down into the wood, or by incising with the skew blade of a knife. It is better not to try to attain full depth on the first

Flat and Level-Surface Carving

The further one gets into wood carving the more interesting it becomes. A good example of a more challenging type of carving is the flat-surface carving shown in Figure 29.

Three steps are involved when undertaking flat-surface carving. If there are long, unbroken outlines in the design, outlining these is most easily and quickly done with a V-tool, or a veiner, but you must be careful not to drive too deeply. The shorter straight lines and quick curves are outlined by driving straight chisels down into the wood just outside these lines (Figure 37). Just enough wood should be left around the design to make final trimming to the exact line possible later on. The third step in the process is to trim away the background to a lower level.

While most professional wood-carvers are trained to carve with chisels exclusively and seldom use knives to do any part of their work, I find that in certain cases substituting a knife for a chisel is advantageous. A knife can at times incise cuts more quickly, especially on soft woods, and it can be easier to maneuver around sharp curves.

Once the design has been outlined with cuts all around, it is best to make short-angled cuts from close to the outline of the design to lower the background. This lessens the danger of inadvertently slicing away parts of the design with low-angled cuts from a greater distance. These can be made later when shoulders have been established to help stop the chisel, should it go out of control.

Once the background has been sliced away to the depth desired—⅛″ is usually enough—then the edges around the design should be carefully trimmed to the lines. Outlines and shoulders of the design should be sharp and clearly defined. The surface of the design is level and flat, as is the background.

Figure 30. An example of low-relief carving.

Carving and Modeling in Low Relief

Carving and modeling in low relief is flat-surface carving carried one step further. The design should first be carefully drawn directly on the wood. All lines should be sharp and easy to see as shown on the comb case project in Figure 30. When this picture was taken, all joinery work, consisting of mortise-and-tenon joints and dovetail joints, had been completed. Only the frame, consisting of stiles and top and bottom rails, had been glued together. Most carving on a piece of this kind should be done before the final assembly. It is much easier to do it then; the pieces can be clamped flat to the top of a workbench, or held in a vise, giving access to all parts of the carving. Sometimes, however, as with the mirror frame shown in Figures 31 and 32, some parts of the carving cannot be completed until after the parts have been glued together. Here, the separate pieces that make a single element

21

Figure 31. Carving a mirror frame with a V-bent tool.

Figure 32. Carving sharp curves using a wooden mallet with a straight chisel.

must first be glued so they line up accurately, before any carving is done. This is particularly apparent in Figure 100. Once the design has been drawn on the wood, the carving is usually started by following the steps suggested earlier in this chapter for doing flat-surface carving.

Figure 33 shows another method of removing waste and lowering the background around a design: using an electric-powered hand router. This timesaving device is highly recommended where its use is practicable, as in this case, where the background areas on the design are quite large and open. This method would not work well on smaller background areas, like those found in the design of the chest for flat tableware.

When you use the electric router, be sure to maintain enough of the surface level of the design so that you can rest the base of the machine on it. Take great care to avoid cutting into the design. One way is to use a cutter with a very small diameter. For the mirror project a $3/16''$ cutter was used. Even with this, stay at a reasonably safe distance from the lines of the design—

as much as $1/8''$ or more. What remains can then be cut out with chisels.

Figure 31 shows a long-bent V-tool being used to cut along the outline of a design before the shaping and modeling which is to come later. The fastest way to outline this kind of work is with chisels, especially when long, unbroken lines need outlining. The blade of the tool is held with the left hand while the right hand pushes it into and through the wood. However, when there are sharper curves or angular areas, there is a better method for outlining and incising, shown in Figure 32, where the straight chisel is hammered into the work with a mallet. In doing these shorter curves, light mallet strokes help to ease the chisel gently around such areas, with less chance of going too far or in the wrong direction. This is the method shown in Figure 34. At other times the handle of the chisel is hit with the palm of the hand, as in Figure 35, but this does not give you as much control over the chisel as tapping it with a mallet will.

Although all of the carving has already been

22

ABOVE *Figure 33.* Using an electric-powered hand router to lower the background and remove waste.

BELOW *Figure 34.* Using light mallet strokes to ease chisel around short curves.

Figure 35. Using palm of hand to hit chisel. This gives the chisel a gentle push, but you actually have less control over the chisel than when using a mallet.

done on the leaf shown in Figures 36, 37, 38, and 39, these views show some of the chisels used to do the modeling after the design has been outlined and the background cleaned up and smoothed. Many times some work on cleaning up a background may be required until the carving is entirely completed. I have even found defects in carving of mine that did not show up until

23

Figure 36.
Figure 37. } Using chisels to do modeling after de-
Figure 38.   sign has been outlined and background
Figure 39.   cleaned up and smoothed.

one or more coats of finish had been applied to the wood.

Small cabinetmaker's hand scrapers are also useful tools; they are very helpful in cleaning up carvings and are especially effective for cleaning and smoothing background areas, provided that the cutting edge of the scraper is small enough to get to them. Their flat steel blades are tempered more or less like handsaws. The cutting edges may be straight or curved and they are sharpened with a fine-tooth mill file. Never use a double-cut file; it won't do the job. After a short bevel has been filed, working the file against the edge, the edge is turned with a burnishing tool, which is a case-hardened, oval-shafted, smooth-bladed tool. If properly used, scrapers smooth better than sandpaper.

Figure 40. Working on sides of a fruit bowl is sometimes easier when it is turned upside down, as in this illustration.

Carving in the Round

Carving in the round entails all of the techniques and methods already described for other types of carving. There are differences, however, because the object being worked is three-dimensional instead of two-dimensional. Carving in the round involves knowing the shapes of things and the proper placement of various elements belonging to the object, such as eyes, ears, legs, fingers, and so on. Human or animal figures often provide the subject matter, but other examples in this category are flame finials on highboys, turned objects like the fruit bowl shown in Figure 130, and the one shown in Figure 40. To do human or animal carving in the round, some elementary knowledge of anatomy is essential.

Objects turned on the lathe may usually be carved while still mounted between the lathe centers. Indeed, if you have a lathe, a good way to hold such objects as models of human figures is to mount them between lathe centers while carving them. Allowing some extra wood at both ends will prevent injury to the figure, and this can be cut off later when the carving is nearly completed. Lathes equipped with an index head, like my lathe in Figure 41, can hold the figure at any one of forty-eight positions while rotating it 360 degrees. Figure 41 shows the candlestick described in Project 13 mounted in the lathe to carve the upper part. Short turnings may be

Figure 41. Lathes with an index-head can rotate the object held 360 degrees. Here a candlestick is mounted while the upper part is carved.

25

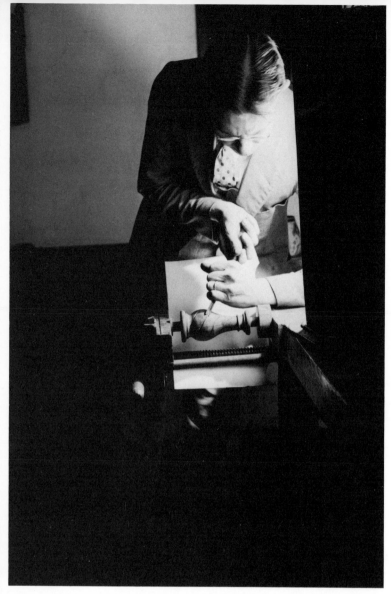

It may seem unimportant to be particularly careful while boasting-in, but it is essential that you not lose the basic shape of the object. Wood lost at this stage is difficult to replace. Most carvings that split or are damaged have to be discarded.

Once this part of the work has been completed, the refining touches bring out those features you wish to emphasize, those refinements that distinguish the work of the individual craftsman. Chisels should be used on three-dimensional carvings whenever any advantage may be gained by doing so. On large carvings, like the one of the Indian in Project 32, chisels are more effective than knives, though for some of the smaller detail work knives may also be used.

Figure 42. Carving the shaft of a bowl fastened between the jaws of a vise.

fastened between the jaws of a vise to carve, like the shaft for the carved bowl shown in Figure 42.

The carving of animal figures in the round has already been fully described in Chapter 1, but a few pertinent points should be repeated, such as the importance of carefully locating and drawing essential details on the block of wood, not only before starting to carve but also when following up with details as the work progresses so nothing essential will be omitted. The center lines should be drawn early, and the location and proportions of the various elements within the design should be carefully considered.

3
Woods and Finishes

Kinds of Wood Suitable for Carving

THE first problem when starting to carve is to select the right kind of wood for the work you want to do from the wide variety of wood available. Some of the woods commonly used are California sugar pine, white pine, yellow poplar, mahogany, cherry, black walnut, oak, chestnut, maple, birch, basswood, red gum, aromatic red cedar, and holly.

The question of procuring suitable lumber to make the things shown in this book is also a matter to which some consideration should be given. Not all of the different kinds of wood we have recommended are available in places where building lumber is sold, and so it becomes necessary to go to other sources of supply.

Among these are firms that specialize in supplying not only lumber but other things a craftsman needs. Most such firms publish catalogs describing the products they sell and give prices. Many advertise in magazines and periodicals in which woodworking or other hobbies are regularly featured. A person using our book would do well to write for catalogs of this kind.

One most helpful periodical of this kind is the bimonthly magazine *Chip Chats,* published by The National Wood Carvers' Association, a nonprofit organization that periodically lists sources of supplies a wood-carver might need. Other good ones are *Fine Woodworking* and *Early American Life,* published by The Early American Society.

PINE

All of the animals shown in Projects 21–29 and the tray in Project 20 were carved from California sugar pine. This wood has no coarse grain and is entirely free of knots. The good grades are soft but not too soft, and they do not have the rubbery or corklike toughness so often found in sapwood of other species. Sharp tools will slice or sever the fibers across the grain almost as smoothly as they will with the grain.

The wood is usually cream-colored but can run from light reddish brown to almost white. It is available in wide planks up to 3″ and even 4″ thick. This makes it an ideal material for carvings for which thick stock is needed. Good kiln-dried stock remains free of checks and other defects to which other woods are subject.

True northern white pine also carves well, if the better, knot-free grades are used. This wood has more distinct grain markings, and though it carves quite well, I consider it a second-choice pine for carving.

YELLOW POPLAR

Yellow poplar, sometimes called tulip poplar, is an excellent soft-textured wood to use for carving. The heartwood is a little harder than pine and carves exceedingly well. Its color runs from pale cream to light and even dark shades of green. Sometimes it is shot through with streaks of dark brown, purple, and even black. Grain markings are often pretty, especially when accentuated by the right finish. Poplar is still relatively inexpensive, and because mature trees develop considerable girth, wide and thick planks are available. Since poplar gives off no resinous flavor, it is a good choice for objects that will come in contact with food and has long been used for making butter molds, cutting boards, dough troughs, and other articles used in preparing or storing food.

MAHOGANY

Mahogany comes in several varieties and grades. The better grades used for carving are heavy and relatively dense and hard. Mahogany from Honduras or Cuba is best; good grades come from Africa; and there is a Mexican variety, though most of this is inferior in quality.

Mahogany is more open-grained than pine or poplar but never too coarse for carving. It has remarkable grain markings and good color qualities, and these, together with an almost ideal texture for carving, make it one of the most popular woods for this purpose. Much of the world's finest furniture is made from mahogany.

The color ranges from pale to deep red browns, with rich orange undertones. Exposure to light and air darkens the wood. Stain accentuates the wood grain, which is often lavishly figured in an endless variety of patterns. Few, if any, other woods can equal its beauty, and I prefer it above all other woods for both wood carving and fine cabinetwork.

CHERRY

Cherry carves exceedingly well and has great beauty. It is harder to carve than mahogany but has beautiful and distinctive grain markings which make it an ideal wood to use for many types of carving. Cherry turns to a deeper red-brown color with the passage of time, whether or not a finish has been applied.

BLACK WALNUT

Black walnut, a harder and tougher wood than either mahogany or cherry, has many of the desirable qualities of both. With sharp tools it carves well. Usually chisels are necessary; but sharp knives will cut it. It runs from medium hard to very hard, and the wood is dense and tough, which makes it ideal for the type of object that has small pieces that might easily break or split off during carving.

The wood is chocolate to purplish brown in color. Creamy sapwood, sometimes found on pieces of walnut, will disappear if the wood is steamed. This is usually done before kiln drying and makes the color more uniform. Walnut is a highly prized cabinet wood for furniture and interior woodwork, and like mahogany it is greatly sought after for making the beautifully figured veneers and carved ornaments to be found on fine period furniture.

OAK

Oak, though hard, carves exceedingly well. It was widely used in earlier times when Gothic motifs were in vogue and would therefore be a proper material to use for building the Gothic chest (Project 7), though black walnut would be equally appropriate. Oak is coarse, with a pronounced pattern of rays that run in streaks throughout the wood. It is therefore a good choice where bold, vigorous patterns constitute the design. It has open pores that require filling when finish is applied. The better grades are quarter-sawed (at a 90-degree angle to the annual rings), making the wood less subject to warping and giving it more beautiful grain markings.

Red oak is gray brown with a reddish cast; white oak is a lighter yellow brown with a grayish cast.

CHESTNUT

Chestnut resembles oak in many respects but is softer and has a coarser grain. Now, because the chestnut blight has killed nearly all the chestnut trees, it is available mostly in boards rescued from old buildings. It is easy to carve, but for most designs where it would be acceptable, oak would do better; chestnut has a coarser grain and the porous areas are softer, so clean, crisp cuts

are more difficult to make than with the harder oak.

ROCK MAPLE

Rock maple is the term used to designate the hardest varieties of this widely used cabinet wood. It is also a popular material for flooring. Rock maple compares with walnut in weight and density. It is strong enough not to split or splinter easily and is excellent for lathe turnings. Its light, creamy color makes it ideal to use in contrast with darker woods, and it is often used to carve chessmen and to make chessboards. It is a fine wood to use for inlay work, for the design or the background. A sharp chisel will cut it clean, leaving crisp and distinct outlines. I used rock maple to carve the top of the chest in Project 8.

BIRCH

The properties of birch are very similar to those of maple; enough so, in fact, that it is sometimes difficult to distinguish one from the other. Birch is a less expensive wood than maple or mahogany, and when stained it can be made to look enough like them that it is frequently used for this purpose. Birch carves well, and because of its light color it can be finished in many different ways.

BASSWOOD

Basswood is sometimes called lin; the tree is an American variety of the European linden which is darker and denser than basswood. The latter is cream-colored, somewhat softer than white pine, with less pronounced grain markings. It carves well and is a favorite with whittlers. Its texture lends itself well to fine detail. It is often used in cheaper grades of furniture, under veneers of more sought-after woods where it shows little or not at all.

RED GUM

Kiln-dried heartwood of red gum is close-grained, so it carves well and is good for wood turning. Thus, it is a good choice for those projects where the turnings are also carved. Avoid gum sapwood, which has a tough, rubber-like texture and is extremely difficult to carve. Red gum is reddish or yellowish brown in color. It warps easily, but if properly seasoned and finished it will hold its shape quite well. When stained it resembles black walnut, though it is much softer and does not have the grain markings found in good walnut.

AROMATIC RED CEDAR

Aromatic red cedar is a good wood to use for carving small figures. This wood would be in much greater demand for both carving and other woodwork if it were not for the numerous knots in cedar boards and logs. Aromatic cedar splits easily; and since a split on the surface may extend deep into the wood, the piece to be used for carving should be closely examined.

Cedar is easy to cut with a knife and has a rich orange-red color, often with contrasting white or cream-colored streaks.

HOLLY

Holly is one of the best woods available for small carvings with very fine detail. Since holly trees seldom attain great size, large blanks are hard to find. It has virtually no grain but has an ivorylike texture and hardness that make it ideal for carving statuettes or small animals. The wood is almost white in color when first cut but darkens to light brown with age.

Finishing

Once a project has been completed, the question of a suitable finish arises. Many carvings need no finish at all. Walnut, a rather durable wood, looks good without any finish, unless left in a damp place where worms might get into it. Cherry and California sugar pine are also often left unfinished.

Many of the projects shown in this book had no finish when they were photographed and could remain like this without seriously affecting either their beauty or their value. In fact, many wood carvings are unsuitably finished, and consequently much of their charm is lost. One of the greatest assets a carving can have, next to good design and workmanship, is its wood grain markings. Therefore, every effort should be made not only to preserve this important feature, but to enhance it if at all possible.

In my opinion very few carvings are improved by covering them with opaque paint. More often than not this only cheapens them. Once they are so mutilated, they might as well have been cast from a mold of some material other than wood, for much of the artistic quality and charm of the work has been lost.

Many craftsmen who love and appreciate the remarkable and wonderful qualities of wood protect and polish their carvings with nothing more than a few coats of wax, rubbed down with a clean, soft cotton cloth. This builds up a smooth sheen without the high gloss or shine of unrubbed varnish finishes.

Boiled linseed oil helps to preserve wood and darkens it. Repeated coats of this, alternated with repeated rubbing and polishing with a soft cloth, will build up a patina on the surface. Some people use oil and wax alternately, rubbing and polishing these to build up the patina more quickly.

If varnish, shellac, lacquer, or other finishes are used, the work must be carefully done to give satisfactory results. One or more coats of shellac, each followed by rubbing the surface with No. 0 or No. 00 steel wool, will build up a surface sheen. The 4-pound cut shellac usually sold should be thinned with not less than an equal amount of denatured alcohol. A greater dilution than this is even better. Shellac should be applied only after all sanding has been carefully done, at a room temperature of at least 70 degrees and in conditions as dust-free as possible. Shellac is not moistureproof, so the final coat should be followed by a coat of wax to protect it.

Varnish builds up a glossy surface much more quickly than shellac and has greater transparency; it is also reasonably moisture-resistant. For these reasons it is preferable to the shellac finish. You can get good results with the better grades of either spar varnish or floor varnish if the first coat or two is reduced with an equal amount of turpentine. Though other thinners are available, and are sometimes recommended, I prefer spirits of turpentine. A longer drying period is necessary for varnish than for shellac. Wait no less than twenty-four hours before again sanding and rubbing the surface with steel wool in preparation for another coat. After enough coats have been applied to build up a gloss, good final results may be obtained in one of two ways: (1) the final coat may be polished down with fine powdered pumice stone and a good paraffin-base rubbing oil, which is available at most good paint stores; or (2) the second, or preferably the third, coat of gloss varnish, this one undiluted, may be followed with a coat of satin gloss varnish. This takes from the surface the objectionable shine of ordinary gloss varnish. This last coat need not be waxed, being quite tough and durable once it has dried.

Lacquer and other synthetic finishing materials are also available. These may be applied with brushes or a sprayer. I suggest first trying such finishes on a piece of wood like the material used on the project if you have not used the finish before.

The beauty and appeal of some projects are enhanced by the use of color. I use paint on carvings very sparingly, and mostly in the form of pigments (the material used to color paint) ground in oil. Burnt umber is a good color to use when staining walnut, pine, and other woods where a brown hue is desired and can be much more inexpensively prepared than buying ready-mixed stain. In fact, I mix nearly all the stains I use by blending and thinning painter's colors ground in oil with turpentine. Bronze powders are available in many colors, including gold. They are mixed with lacquer thinner or vehicles recommended by the manufacturer and can be applied with artist's brushes. I add a small amount of varnish to the mixture, which makes it stick better to the wood, but too much varnish will change the color so it should be added in very small amounts. Coats of varnish over the bronze powder paint will fade the colors and in most cases are not needed.

The stain I prefer for mahogany is orange red in hue. It's an expensive stain, probably because the dyes used to make it consist of expensive materials; the manufacturers from whom I had been accustomed to buy it have stopped making it. Fortunately, the most pleasing red color for mahogany I have found can be achieved by white-washing the mahogany with slaked lime, exactly as people used to whitewash fences. Lime applied to mahogany in this way reacts chemically, coloring the mahogany a rich orange red, but it does not react this way with any other wood. It is therefore an ideal coloring agent for mahogany furniture inlaid with other kinds of wood or furniture veneered with marquetry. Remove every trace of the lime after the mahogany has been colored in this way with a thin mixture of boiled linseed oil and turpentine. Succeeding finishing coats may then be applied over this.

To achieve a smooth surface on open-grained

woods like oak, mahogany, chestnut, and walnut, you must fill the open pores before finishing coats like varnish are applied. Silex filler in paste or liquid form, thinned with turpentine to the consistency of heavy cream, can be rubbed into the pores with the fingers or with a soft cotton cloth. All residue left on the surface must be removed as soon as this mixture starts to set and thicken, or it will form such a tough crust that it can be removed only by scraping or vigorous sanding. If large surfaces are to be filled, do small areas at a time, since the filler dries quickly.

Another effective way to color carved objects is to use artist's watercolors since they do not obscure wood grain to any great degree. Watercolors are easy to apply, and you can easily mix them to achieve almost any color you wish. The use of watercolors is restricted, however, to light-hued woods like pine, basswood, holly, birch, and poplar, and better results are achieved when they are applied to the softer woods that absorb them better. Watercolors are seldom used on dark-hued woods like walnut, mahogany, or cherry since the colors do not show up on them.

4

Projects

Patterns for Carving

PATTERNS for a few carvings are shown full size; most have been drawn over graph squares. Each graph square represents 1″ on the actual carving. The lines of the squares are numbered vertically and horizontally to help you locate positions when redrawing the pattern to size. To reduce or enlarge the dimensions of the carving itself, you can change the scale: a square can equal ½″, 2″, or whatever size you wish.

The other numbers indicated on the drawings of the animals represent thicknesses in sixteenths of an inch. Thus the figure 8 indicates a thickness at that spot of $\frac{8}{16}$″, or ½″; 50 indicates a thickness of $\frac{50}{16}$″, or $3\frac{1}{8}$″. These dimensions were

taken from the carved object with calipers. There
is no need to adhere to a thickness exactly, but it
is there to help you arrive at a close approxima-
tion of the correct thickness.

Types of Wood

I have indicated what kind of wood was used
on each project, except for the ten animals at the
end, which are all made of California sugar pine.
The photographs will show which way the grain
goes.

Project 1
Cutting Board

The cutting board shown in Figure 43 is part of a collection of old wood carvings. The asymmetry of the pattern and of the board itself indicates an amateur carver—and adds to its charm. I assume that the greater part of the design was carved with knives but I cannot say for sure. Chisels would certainly help to make the job easier.

The drawing of the design in Figure 44 eliminates some of the imperfections of the original and shows enough detail that the design can be duplicated with reasonable authenticity. In doing such carvings, you need not try to duplicate the imperfections found on the original, since the idea is not to make an antique but to use the design.

The wood used is yellow poplar.

Figure 43.

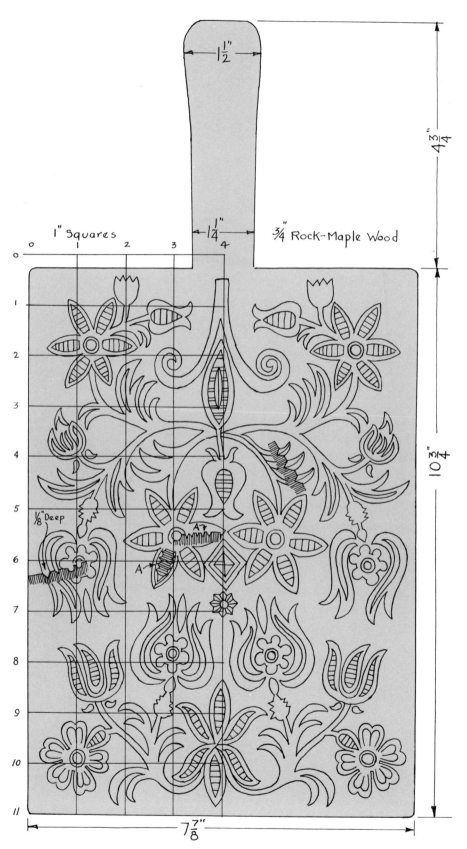

Figure 44.

Project 2
Wastebasket

A bit of carving adds beauty even to quite simple objects. The wastebasket shown in Figure 45 is easy to make. Woodworking machinery is not required, though of course it would help. Simpler butt joints could be substituted for the kind shown, and all of these could be made with hand tools. Good woods to use are yellow poplar, walnut, cherry, or mahogany.

Carving the four panels presents no great problems; the flowers are a little more difficult than the leaves. The background areas on this project are large enough that a lot of the routing-out could be done with an electric-powered hand router, but hand tools can do the job almost as quickly. As suggested in Chapter 1, the background areas, once they are cut down, can be given an interesting texture with punches. The shaded part of the background in Figure 46 shows how this might look.

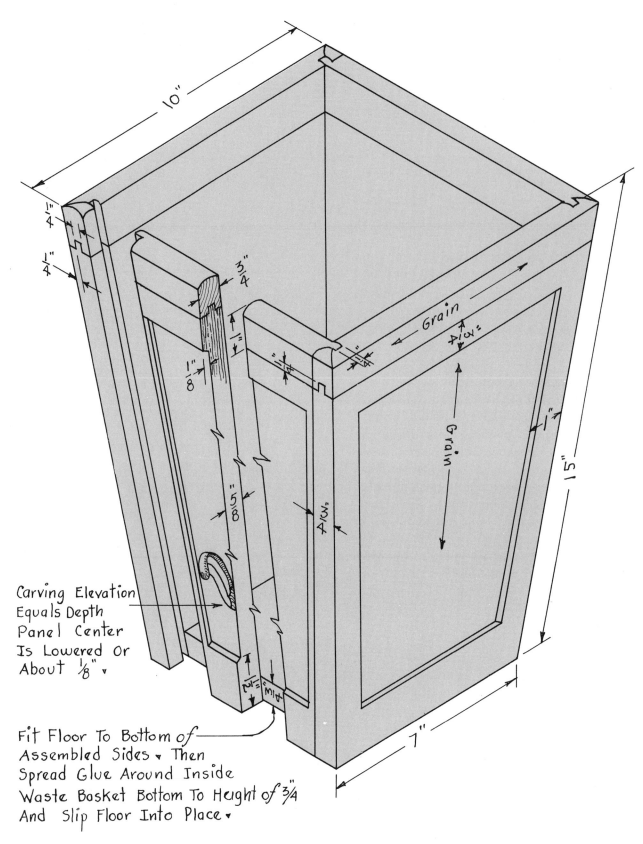

10"

$\frac{1}{4}$"

$\frac{1}{4}$"

$\frac{3}{4}$"

$\frac{1}{8}$"

$\frac{1}{8}$"

$\frac{5}{8}$"

Grain

Grain

15"

1"

7"

Carving Elevation
Equals Depth
Panel Center
Is Lowered Or
About $\frac{1}{8}$".

Fit Floor To Bottom of
Assembled Sides . Then
Spread Glue Around Inside
Waste Basket Bottom To Height of $\frac{3}{4}$"
And Slip Floor Into Place .

Figure 45.

1" Squares

Figure 46.

Project 3
Carved Bookends

ardous and I hesitate to recommend it. The steel rods are easy to use; any machine shop can supply them.

Figures 49, 50, 53, and 54 show all the details necessary to reproduce these designs.

The bookends shown in Figure 47 are made of oak. The tendency today is to use more exotic woods, such as mahogany, walnut, or teak, for decorative objects like these. However, few woods have the rugged characteristics of oak, and for designs with a bold figure and not much fine detail it is an excellent material. Not only the design but the grain pattern as well contribute to the beauty of the object.

Another design suitable for oak is the one in Figure 50. It has the same type of bold pattern that would look good on this coarse-grained wood.

Figure 47, however, could also be done in a smoother material than oak, and designs like those shown in Figures 51 and 52 definitely require a finer-grained wood, like mahogany or walnut.

The design in Figure 51 is classical, and here I recommend mahogany to accomplish most successfully the fine detail work in the shell carved in a hollowed-out niche.

Three of these parts of bookends are fitted and screwed to metal plates underneath to hold them upright. The other two, carved of mahogany (Figures 51 and 52), are weighted by drilling two 1″ holes deep into the bottom of each and then inserting short steel rods. These rods are then held in place by the baseboards screwed to the bottom of each bookend. It is easier to weight them this way than to pour melted hot lead into the holes. I once used hot lead weighting with good results, but this method is somewhat haz-

Figure 47. Oak has a rough, distinctive grain suitable for bold designs.

Figure 48.

Figure 49.

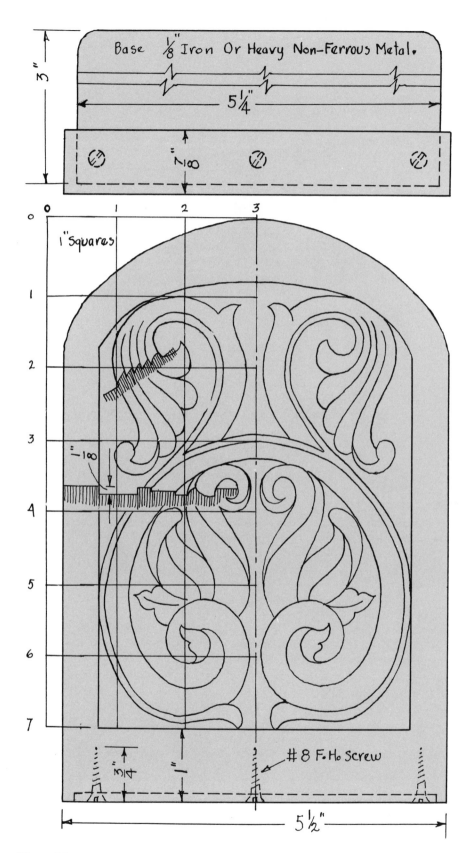

Base ⅛" Iron Or Heavy Non-Ferrous Metal.

3"

5¼"

⅛"

0   1   2   3

1" squares

1   2   3   4   5   6   7

⅛"

#8 F. H. Screw

¾"

1"

5½"

Figure 50.

Figure 51. Two bookends (above and facing page)
carved in mahogany. Designs like these require the
finer grain of this wood.

Figure 52.

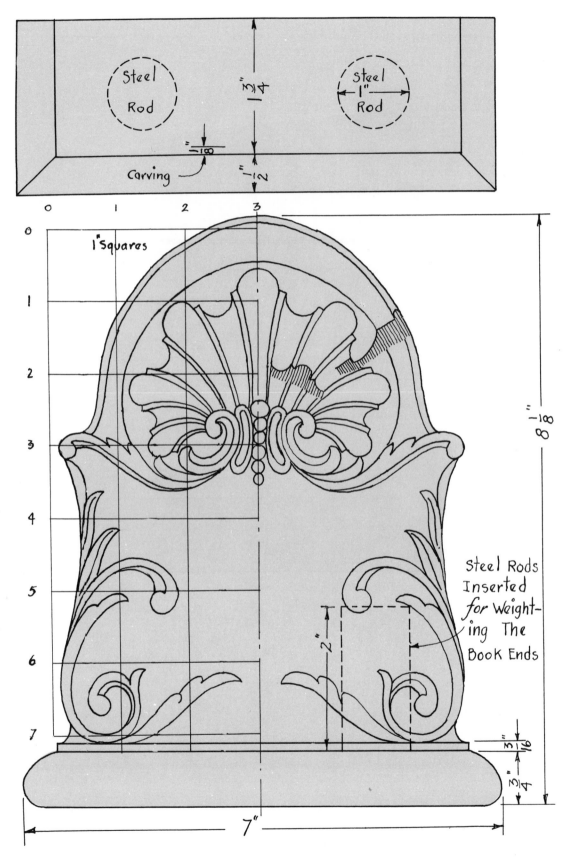

Figure 53.

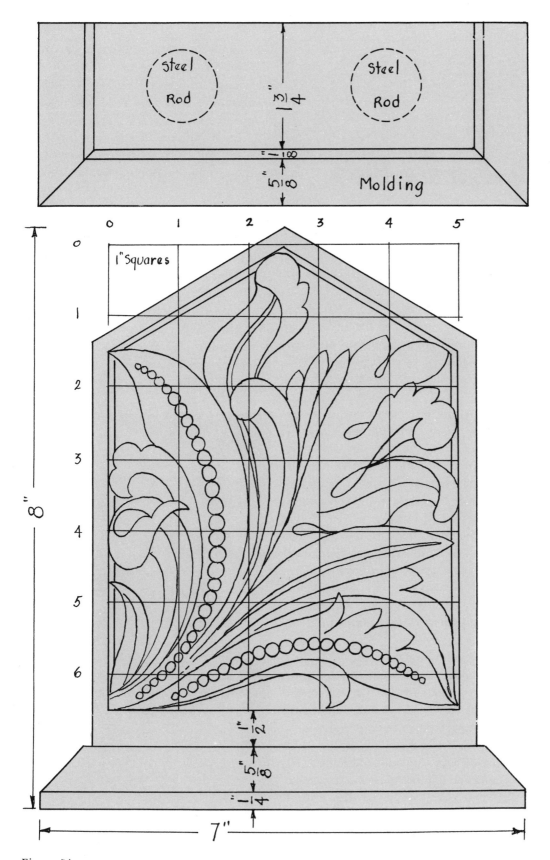

Steel Rod

Steel Rod

$1\frac{3}{4}"$

$\frac{1}{8}"$

$\frac{5}{8}"$

Molding

0   1   2   3   4   5

0

1"Squares

1

2

3

4

5

6

$\frac{1}{2}"$

$\frac{5}{8}"$

$\frac{1}{4}"$

8"

7"

Figure 54.

Project 4
Chip-Carved Box

The chip-carved box shown in Figures 56 and 57 is about the size of the old Bible boxes, now so greatly prized by antique collectors.

The wood used is mahogany. In addition to the carving and inlay banding on the lid, the box is decorated with pierced metal mounts on three sides, cut from a sheet of 18-gauge pewter. These are sawed to shape with a jeweler's saw (Figure 55).

Figures 58, 58A, and 58B show construction details. Grooves for the splined miter joints at each corner may be cut on the table saw and should be kept well back from the outside surfaces to avoid cutting into them when carving the stars on the corners of the box. If you do not have a power saw, the corners may be put together with glue and brads, but the brads should be hidden under the strips around the base. Where the holes over the nail heads are apt to show they should be filled with little wooden plugs trimmed from a stick.

Bar clamps pull these mitered joints together tightly so they fit snugly.

Notice in the cross-section view that the bottom edges of sides and ends are rabbeted to allow room for the floor, which is held in place with glue and brads.

The stars on each corner can be carved almost completely before gluing the sides, though some touching up will have to be done afterward.

After planing and sanding the board to be used for the top, lay out the star design. Also cut out the grooves for the inlay banding. I did not have an electric hand router like the one shown in Figure 33 when the box was made, so I cut the grooves with a knife and a narrow chisel. A small chest lock can be put on the box before the sides are assembled.

The metal mounts may be dispensed with, but they add interest to the design. Sheet pewter is composed now of a large percentage of tin and so is fairly soft. This makes it easy to saw with metal-cutting jeweler's saw blades. After sawing the outside to shape, drill small holes at places on the inside that have to be cut out. Since this kind of saw blade cuts on the down stroke, it works best if you sit well below the level of the handle. Such sawing can also be done on a small jigsaw; this works better if you wax the blade occasionally during use.

Any finish you may want to put on the chest should be applied before the metal mounts are nailed on the box with brass escutcheon pins.

ABOVE *Figure 55.* Sawing pierced metal mounts to shape with a jeweler's saw.

OPPOSITE TOP *Figure 56.* Chip-carved box made of mahogany (front) and decorated with pierced metal mounts.

OPPOSITE BOTTOM *Figure 57.* Chip-carved box (rear).

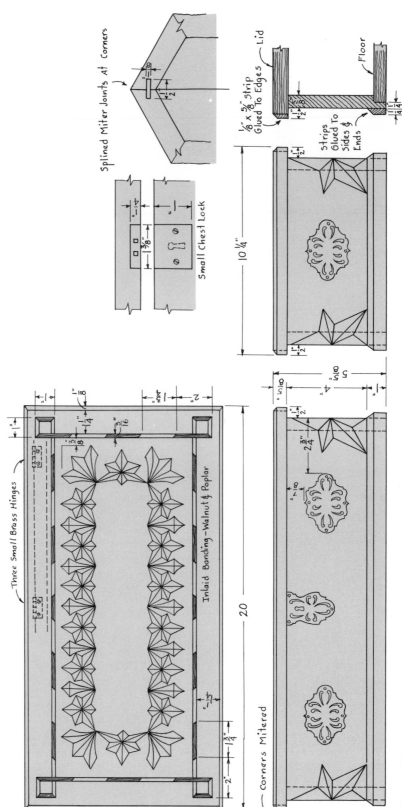

Splined Miter Joints At Corners

Small Chest Lock

1/8" x 5/8" Strip
Glued To Edges

Lid

Strips Glued To
Sides & Ends

Floor

10 1/4"

Three Small Brass Hinges

Inlaid Banding - Walnut & Poplar

20

Corners Mitered

Figure 58.

metal Mounts

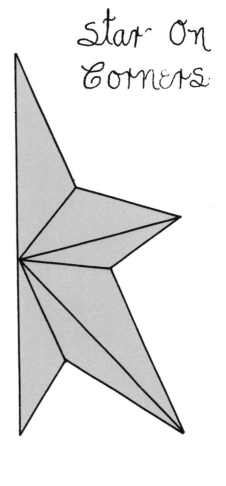

star On Corners

Figure 58A.

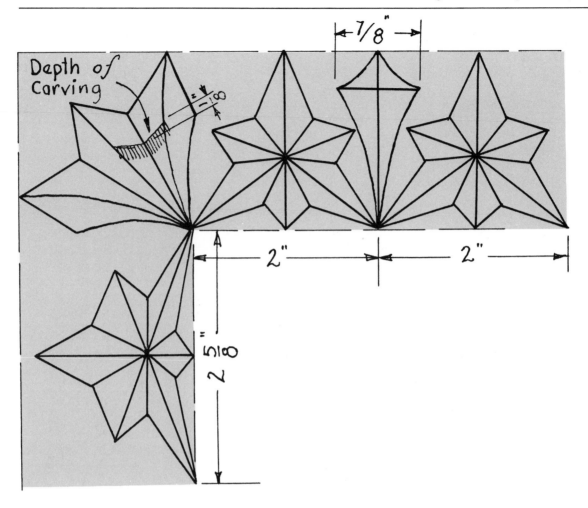

Figure 58B.

Project 5
Carved Box with Bird Design

Boxes and small chests have always intrigued me because there are so many ways to embellish and decorate them—and they are, of course, useful. I carved the one shown here of cherry wood to give to my granddaughter.

The corners are dovetailed. Dovetailing looks best when the tails are wider than the pins, the way hand-cut dovetails were nearly always made before machines were used to do it. Such dovetailing is found on drawers of custom-made furniture and in other quality pieces.

Figure 63 shows the layout for dovetails on this box. First the tail members should be sawed to shape, on a band saw if you have one, as shown in Figure 61. After sawing carefully on the waste area to the line, what little smoothing and trimming is needed can be done quickly with a thin file and chisel. Lay this cutout tail section over the pin section to which it is to be joined and draw the lines for cutting the pin members. Then with a try square extend these lines back to the line indicating the depth of the saw cuts which are shown being made with a dovetail saw in Figure 62.

When the sawing shown in Figure 62 has been done, most of the waste on the pin member can be sawed out with repeated cuts made close together on the band saw. Be sure when doing this to have the waste marked with an X (see Figure 62) to eliminate the possibility of sawing off parts

of the pins. The remainder of the waste can easily be removed with a coping saw.

Figure 64 illustrates a useful type of protractor for laying out dovetails. It adjusts to any angle; the leg of the protractor can be moved about easily by loosening the thumbscrew and held in place by tightening it.

The lid of this small box can be rabbeted to fit down into the top of the box as shown in Figure 63, or it can be left flat on the underside and fastened to the box with small brass hinges.

To carve the lid, first draw the design on ordinary paper, then transfer it to the wood with carbon paper. Darken these lines with a narrow-tipped felt marking pen so all outlines are clearly visible. V-tools and other carving chisels are then used to outline various parts of the design and to prepare to lower the background. Shape the bird, leaves, flowers, and vines either while cutting out the background or, if you prefer, after all of the background has been lowered and cleaned up.

Figure 59. Carved and dovetailed box with bird design (front).

TOP *Figure 60.* A full view of the bird design.

ABOVE LEFT *Figure 61.* Sawing tail members to shape on a band saw.

ABOVE RIGHT *Figure 62.* Using dovetail saw to cut pin members; the waste is marked with an X.

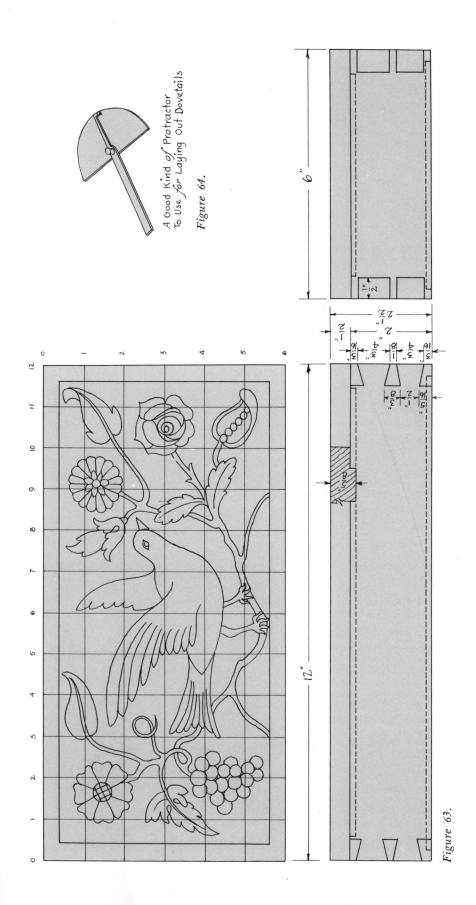

A Good Kind of Protractor
To Use for Laying Out Dovetails

Figure 64.

Figure 63.

Project 6
Sculptured Box

Three views of another very interesting carved box are shown in Figures 65, 66, 67, 68, 69, and 70. Not only is the top of this box flamboyantly carved over its entire surface, but all four sides are sawed and shaped to interesting contours. This box, like the one with the bird on the lid, is made with cherry wood, and the grain markings add much to its beauty.

This type of carving has an eighteenth-century, French rococo feeling. While this box may seem a complicated, time-consuming thing to make and carve, it actually can be done rather easily by anyone with even a small amount of experience. The leaves and scrolls are cut with long sweeps of the tool. Beads may take a little more time but are worth it because they add interesting accents to the design. Some directions for carving these beads will be found on page 19.

Corner joints were made on this box with dovetails, as was done on the box in Project 5. The dovetailing adds a handsome note of distinction, even after the sides have been sawed to shape.

This sawing on the sides of the box is done only after the lid has been fitted and carved, so that the lid and sides can be sawed simultaneously. Some trimming and smoothing must then be done with chisels, files, and sandpaper.

Care should be taken in the final trimming to keep the shape of curves nicely rounded. It will help if the wood-carver moves some distance away from the carving from time to time, to examine it from another vantage point. It is also helpful to turn the carving and view it from different directions. I have found that flaws in a carving and awkward shaping will often show up clearly in a photograph—flaws that were not so obvious when the work itself was examined. Perhaps this is because the shadows that show up on a photograph highlight the flaw.

Some sanding is usually required to clean up carvings like these, though it can be kept to a minimum if tools are sharp and the work is done carefully.

Carving of the kind that is on this box can be finished in many different ways. Wax alone can be used, or boiled linseed oil and wax, well rubbed and polished. Stain and varnish can also be used. However there are possibilities for doing much more than this and your artistic talents can be given full play by using colors in oil or artist's colors, rubbed on sparingly as suggested in Chapter 3. Dusting with gold bronze powders around deep crevices and along rows of beads while the colors are still wet accentuates these areas. If woods like pine, poplar, or basswood are used, where grain markings are not to be a decorative feature, more lavish use of color is possible.

Figure 65.   The flamboyantly carved top.

Figure 66. The sides of the box are carved to fit the
edges of the top.

Figure 67. The grain markings of the cherry wood
add much to the beauty of the box.

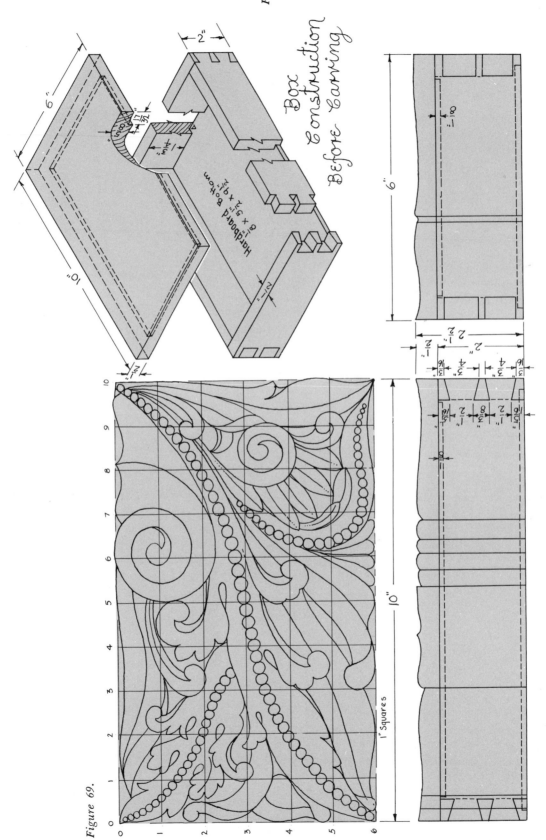

Figure 68.

Box Construction
Before Carving

Hardboard Bottom
⅛″ × 5½″ × 9½″

Figure 69.

1″ Squares

Figure 70.

Walnut or oak are the two appropriate kinds of wood to use when building a chest of this early period style.

Project 7
Gothic Chest

One of the more ambitious projects in this book is the Gothic chest shown in Figure 71. For anyone who would like to build a hand-carved chest and who seeks a design worthy of his best efforts, this might just meet his requirements. The traditional linenfold carving is used for the center panel in the front and the two end panels. Figure 73 illustrates the delicate panels on either side of the center one.

The carved tracery on the bottom and top rails on the front of the chest may also be used on the top and bottom rails on both ends. No carving of any kind need be done on the back of the chest.

Panels and rails should be carved before parts of the chest are glued together. However, all joints and other cabinet-work on the chest should be prepared before carving is started. The heavier tracery should be carved first. Smooth the background around the heavy tracery, all to a level $\frac{3}{16}''$ below the surface of the board, and then lay out the patterns for the narrower tracery and the floral inserts. The different levels are indicated in the cross-section view in Figure 75.

The Gothic tracery on the rails is carved like the bottom $\frac{3}{16}''$ level of the panels. Patterns for the panels and rails can be reproduced from Figures 74 and 76. Patterns for carving the linenfold panel are shown in Figures 77 and 78 and rosette patterns in Figure 79. Construction details for building the chest are shown in Figure 72.

Figure 71.

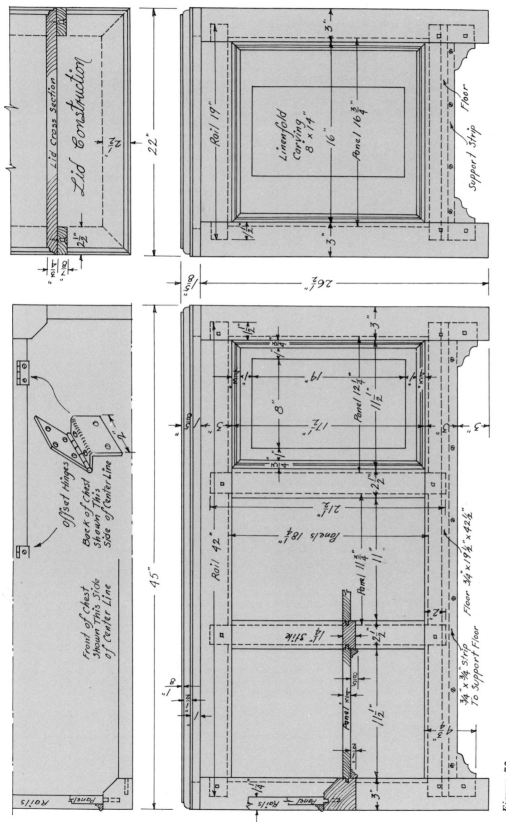

Figure 72.

Figure 73. The delicate side panels of the front of
Gothic chest.

1" Squares

Pattern for Panel Gothic Chest.

Figure 74.

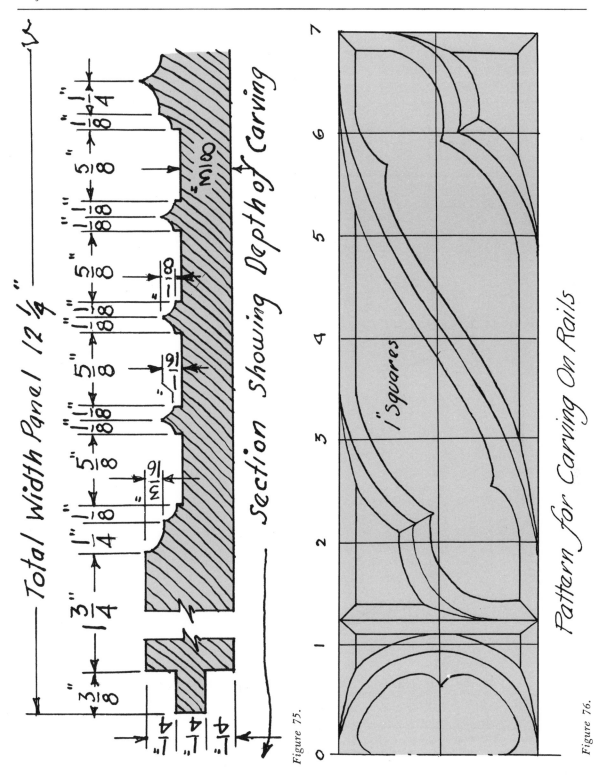

Total Width Panel 12½"

3" $\frac{3}{8}$

3" $1\frac{3}{4}$

1" $1\frac{1}{4}$

1" $\frac{5}{8}$

1" $1\frac{1}{8}$

5" $\frac{5}{8}$

1" $1\frac{1}{8}$

5" $\frac{5}{8}$

1" $1\frac{1}{8}$

5" $\frac{5}{8}$

1" $1\frac{1}{8}$

5" $\frac{5}{8}$

1" $1\frac{1}{8}$

1" $1\frac{1}{8}$

$\frac{3}{16}$"

$\frac{1}{16}$"

$\frac{1}{8}$"

$\frac{3}{8}$"

1" $\frac{1}{4}$ 1" $\frac{1}{4}$ 1" $\frac{1}{4}$

Section Showing Depth of Carving

Figure 75.

1" Squares

Pattern for Carving On Rails

Figure 76.

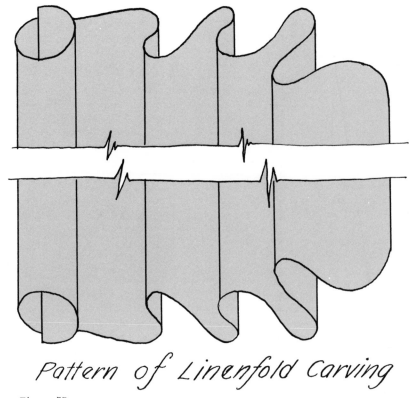

Pattern of Linenfold Carving

Figure 77.

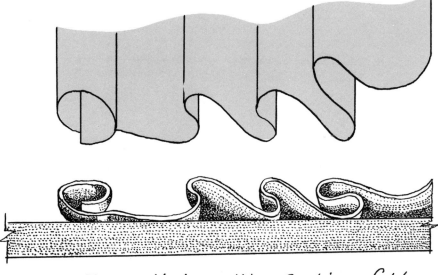

Shows Undercutting On Linenfold

Figure 78.

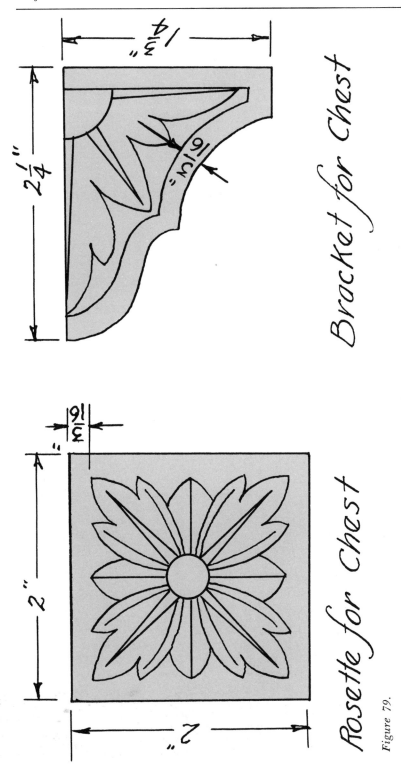

Bracket for Chest

1 3/4"

2 1/4"

.6 cm

Rosette for Chest

3/16

1"

2"

2"

Figure 79.

Project 8
Chest for Flat Tableware

Figures 80 to 83 show the inside and the outside of a small chest to hold flat tableware. Building it involves a bit of cabinetmaking first, as you can see when you examine the drawings.

Essentially, it is simply a box with a lid and a drawer, within which there are racks to hold the tableware. The board for the top of the lid should be planed and made ready for the transfer of the pattern, which is reproduced in Figures 90, 91, and 92. This may seem like an intricate design, but it is less complicated than it seems when drawn on the chest top, where it is repeated four times to complete the design. I used maple, and was able to carve it in three days.

Our working drawings show how to line the chest with felt cloth, but there is another lining known as Suede-tex. It is blown on with a flocking gun, leaving the surface with a velvety velour finish.

Suede-tex comes in a variety of colors, and adhesive to match each color is available. To coat the inside of the chest with Suede-tex, first brush the adhesive onto a surface. Load the gun with Suede-tex and spray it evenly over the surface to coat it. Any of the fibers that do not stick to the adhesive may be retrieved and used again on another job. Suede-tex, adhesive, thinner to clean the paintbrush or reduce the adhesive, and flocking gun may be purchased from supply houses that sell art or craft and hobby supplies.

For those who prefer the longer lasting and thicker felt lining, follow the directions given in Figures 84, 85, 86, 87, 88, and 89. Elmer's Glue or other quick-setting glues may be used; some clamping to hold the felt in place may have to be done until the glue sets.

Elmer's Glue, when used for this purpose, should be thinned with water and a first coat brushed on. Allow this to dry until it becomes tacky and then brush on a second coat of glue of normal consistency. The glue should be applied both to the wood and to the felt.

Figure 80. Chest for flat tableware (front).

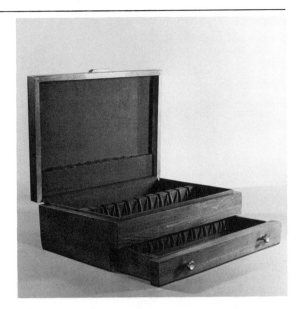

Figure 81. The carved top of the tableware chest.

Figure 82. Two views of the interior of the table-
Figure 83. ware chest.

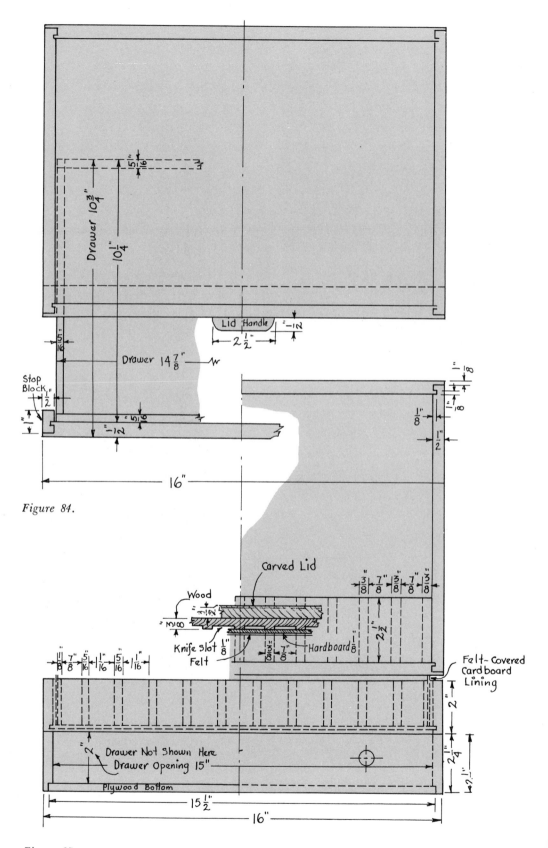

Figure 84.

Figure 85.

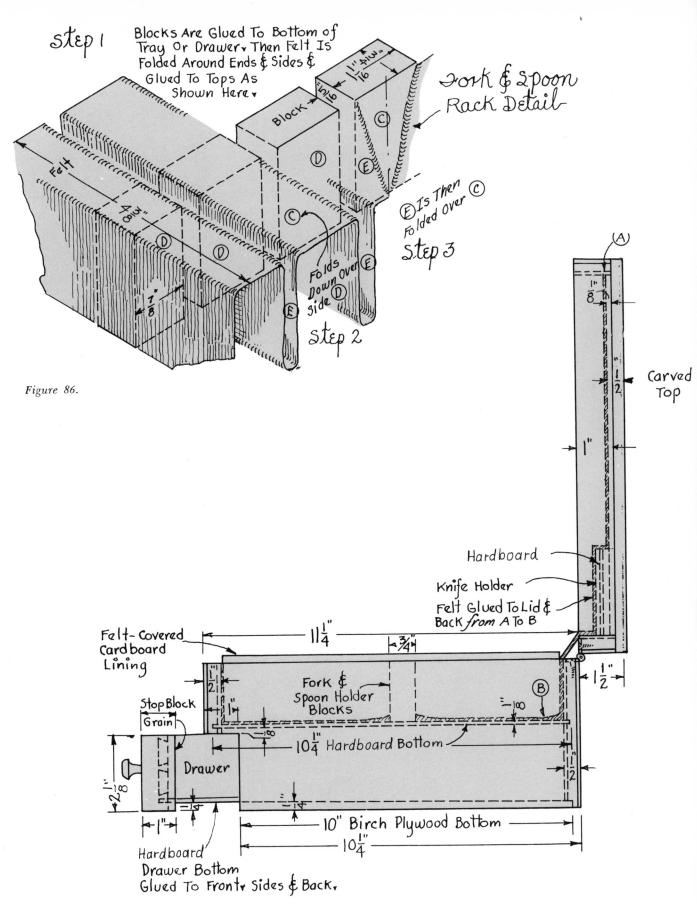

Step 1

Blocks Are Glued To Bottom of Tray Or Drawer. Then Felt Is Folded Around Ends & Sides & Glued To Tops As Shown Here.

Fork & Spoon Rack Detail

Block

$\frac{15}{16}$

$1\frac{1}{16}''$

C

D

E

E Is Then Folded Over C

Step 3

Felt

$4\frac{3}{16}''$

D

D

$\frac{1}{8}''$

C

Folds Down Over side

E

D

E

Step 2

Figure 86.

A

$\frac{1}{8}''$

$1\frac{1}{2}''$

1"

Carved Top

Hardboard

Knife Holder

Felt Glued To Lid & Back from A To B

Felt-Covered Cardboard Lining

$11\frac{1}{4}''$

$\frac{3}{4}''$

$1\frac{1}{2}''$

$1\frac{1}{2}''$

1"

Fork & Spoon Holder Blocks

B

$\frac{1}{8}''$

$10\frac{1}{4}''$ Hardboard Bottom

$\frac{1}{2}''$

Stop Block

Grain

$\frac{1}{8}''$

Drawer

$2\frac{1}{8}''$

$\frac{1}{4}''$

1"

$\frac{1}{4}''$

10" Birch Plywood Bottom

$10\frac{1}{4}''$

Hardboard Drawer Bottom Glued To Front, Sides & Back.

Figure 87.

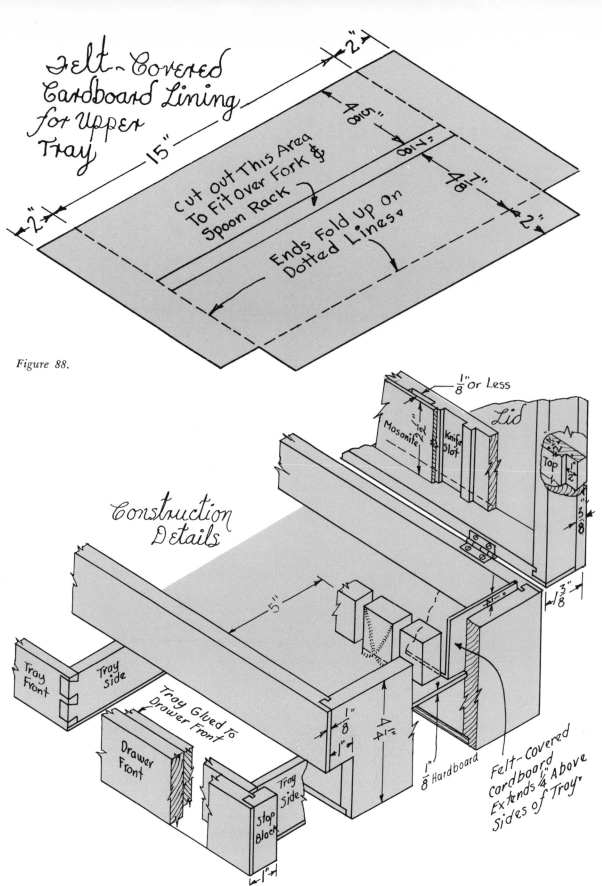

Felt-Covered
Cardboard Lining
for Upper
Tray

15"

2"

2"

Cut Out This Area
To Fit Over Fork &
Spoon Rack

Ends Fold Up On
Dotted Lines

4 5/16"

1 1/8"

4 7/8"

2"

Figure 88.

Construction
Details

1/8" Or Less

Lid

Masonite

Knife
Slot

Top 1 1/2"

3/8

1 3/8"

5"

1/8"

4 1/4"

1"

1/8" Hardboard

Felt-Covered
cardboard
Extends 1/4" Above
Sides of Tray.

Tray
Front

Tray
Side

Tray Glued To
Drawer Front

Drawer
Front

Tray
Side

Stop
Block

1"

Figure 89.

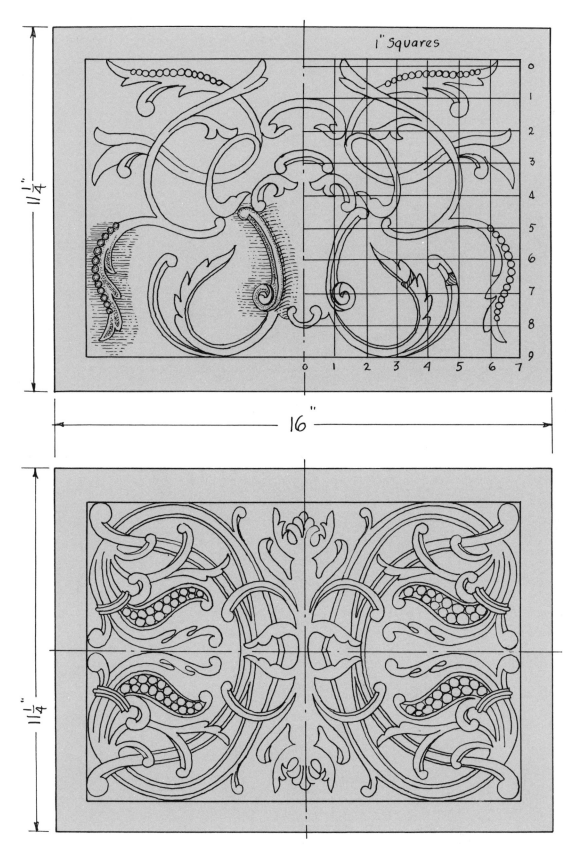

1" Squares

Figure 90.

Figure 91.

Figure 92.

Project 9
Picture Frames

A good picture deserves a good frame—one that is eye-catching and beautiful in a way that does not detract from the picture itself.

The carving on the frames in Figures 93 and 94 is decorative and at the same time unobtrusive enough to allow us to enjoy the painting. Details showing how to make and carve these two frames are given in Figures 95 through 99.

The size of the picture sometimes helps to determine the width of the framing material. Good proportions add a great deal to the viewer's pleasure and should therefore be carefully considered. No hard and fast rule can be applied here; large pictures are sometimes framed with narrow moldings and vice versa. The main problem is overdecorated frames that compete with the picture.

The picture of the village blacksmith measures 18″ by 24″, and the hand-carved molding is 2⅛″ wide. The dog picture is a framed Christmas card, and here the carved molding is a bit wider to allow for some distinctive carving.

Good woods, especially if the frame is painted, are poplar or white pine.

Figure 93. Carved picture frame.

Figure 94. This picture frame has a wider molding
to allow for some distinctive carving.

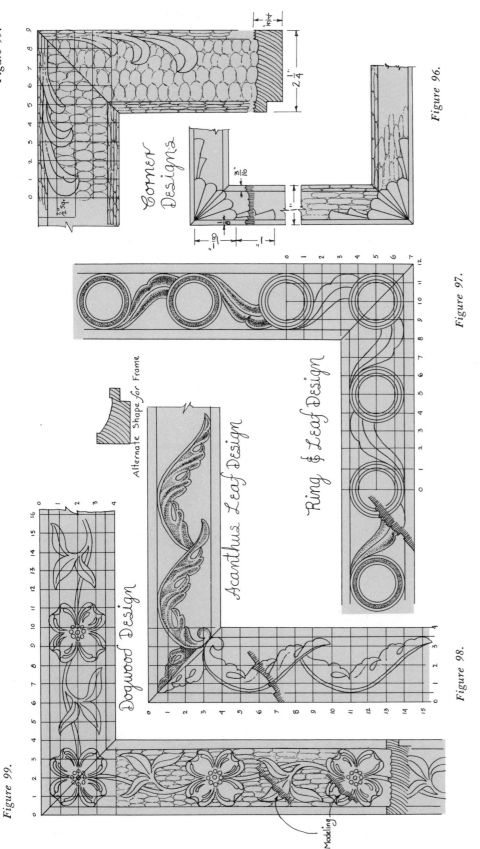

Figure 95.

Figure 96.

Corner Designs

Figure 97.

Ring & Leaf Design

Figure 98.

Alternate Shape for Frame

Acanthus Leaf Design

Dogwood Design

Modeling

Figure 99.

Project 10
Walnut Mirror Frame

The mirror frame shown in Figure 101 was made of black walnut. It is 19″ wide and 31″ high and was made from 7/8″-thick stock.

Working drawings showing layouts for the patterns used to saw the pieces to shape, join the parts together, and make layouts to do the carving are shown in Figures 102, 103, 104, and 105. Mortise-and-tenon joints hold the four pieces together, and as you can see in Figure 105 these are made closer to the back than to the front of the frame, so there is no danger of cutting into them when doing the carving.

If a dado head on the table saw is used to cut the tenons on the top rail, it will be necessary to saw the top rail lengthwise into two 4″-wide pieces and then glue them back together after the tenons have been cut and fitted to the mortises in the side pieces (see Figure 103). However, if the tenons are made with hand tools, this will not be necessary.

Figure 100 shows mortises and tenons made, most of the carving done, and the parts ready to be glued together. Some carving at the joints is left undone to be completed when the sections have been glued together, so that all parts of the design can be properly lined up.

Figure 33 in Chapter 2 shows how to remove the background area with an electric-powered hand router. It also shows that some of the waste around the edges was left intact in order to support the bed of the router and to keep the area being routed out at an even keel. What waste is left can easily be chiseled off later. Also, because

the router bit does not cut the background absolutely smooth, some of this can be made smoother with a router plane.

I do not advise using a router bit more than 3/16″ in diameter. This will allow you to get into tight corners without as great a likelihood of cutting into the design. When the power router is being used, try to stay at least 1/8″ away from the parts that are to be carved later. This will give you enough wood to do nice modeling on the design.

The shell at the top is carved at a level lower than the background around it. Therefore the pattern for the shell should not be drawn until most of the other carving around it has been done. Notice also, in Figure 100, that some band sawing is not yet done at the top and the bottom of the stiles. These parts are left straight so that clamps may be used there to pull the frame together when the joints are glued.

Plate glass for a mirror is 1/4″ thick and quite heavy. I used Masonite for backing against the mirror, but plywood can also be used. Because of the weight of the mirror, strong wire should be used, and the wire should be fastened securely to the frame. I used two metal mending plates, with one end slightly turned up. These were fastened with wood screws to the back of the frame, and the wire was fastened to them.

ABOVE *Figure 100.* Walnut mirror frame with mortises and tenons made, most of the carving done, and parts ready to be glued together.

Figure 101. Walnut mirror frame. Mortise-and-tenon
joints hold the four pieces together.

Figure 103.

Figure 102.

Figure 104.

Figure 105.

In Order To Make
It Easier To Cut
The Tenons On The
Power Saw ~ Rip Into
Two 4" Pieces ~
Cut Tenons On Both
Ends of The Lower
Half of This Top ~
Then Glue The Two
Halves Back Together.

Top $\frac{7}{8}$" x 8" x 20"
Two Sides $\frac{7}{8}$" x $3\frac{3}{8}$" x 25"
Bottom $\frac{7}{8}$" x $5\frac{3}{8}$" x 16"
Mirror 14" x 18"

1" Squares

Mirror

14"

18"

8"

4"

$1\frac{1}{2}$"

$\frac{1}{2}$"

$5\frac{3}{8}$"

$1\frac{1}{2}$"

$\frac{7}{8}$"

A

B

Mirror

$\frac{3}{16}$"

$\frac{3}{8}$"

$\frac{11}{16}$"

$\frac{7}{8}$"

$3\frac{3}{8}$"

$18\frac{1}{2}$"

$2\frac{5}{8}$"

Tenon

Project 11
Kitchen Mirror

What more appropriate theme could you pick for the design of a small kitchen mirror than the coffee mill, the pot, and the steaming cup of brew? I have already discussed in Project 4 how bits of ornamental metalwork can be used to enhance a carving. In this instance, metal, wood (poplar), glass, wood carving, and color are combined to make a useful object beautiful.

To make the frame, first cut and fit the strips of wood together, as shown in Figure 107. Before assembling them with glue and brads, rabbet the edges in the back to hold the mirror, and also the metal in the upper section. Draw the pattern for the carved borders of the frame on paper and transfer these to the assembled frame with carbon paper. Then cut down the background to a depth of a little more than $\frac{1}{16}''$ with carving chisels.

The pattern for the copper cutout is taken from Figure 109 and should be drawn or pasted on the copper sheet. I used 20-gauge copper for this so it would be heavy enough not to buckle when laid flat against the metal background under it. Thinner metal can be glued to other metal with epoxy. When I made this mirror, epoxy-type glue was not yet available, so using the heavier metal was a necessary precaution.

In the description of the chip-carved box I showed how a jeweler's saw is used to cut nonferrous sheet metal. Small holes are drilled first, mostly in the corners of waste areas. The saw blade is inserted through these holes and then fastened into the jeweler's saw frame. These blades are very thin but quite strong, and if carefully used one blade should saw out every piece of waste on this project without breaking. The blade cuts on the down stroke so you should sit low enough so that the saw handle can be pulled down without bending or twisting the blade on the cutting stroke. Jeweler's saws are available in most hobby and art supply stores or from firms that supply equipment for jewelers.

The copper can be polished with very fine steel wool or can be cleaned with pickling solution, which is a watered-down sulfuric acid, approximately one part acid to fifteen parts water. If you prepare your own pickling solution, be sure to pour the acid slowly and carefully into the water, not the other way around. Store it in

Figure 106. The kitchen mirror combines metal, wood, glass, wood carving, and color.

a covered earthenware or enamelware container
when not in use.

After rinsing the pickling solution off the
copper with cold water under a faucet and drying
the copper with a clean cloth, you are ready to
glue it to the background metal and fasten it
to the frame. Screw a piece of thin plywood or
Masonite to the back of the frame to hold both
it and the mirror in place, as shown in Figure
108. The outside edges of the frame are painted
with several coats of paint in order to disguise
the different layers of materials.

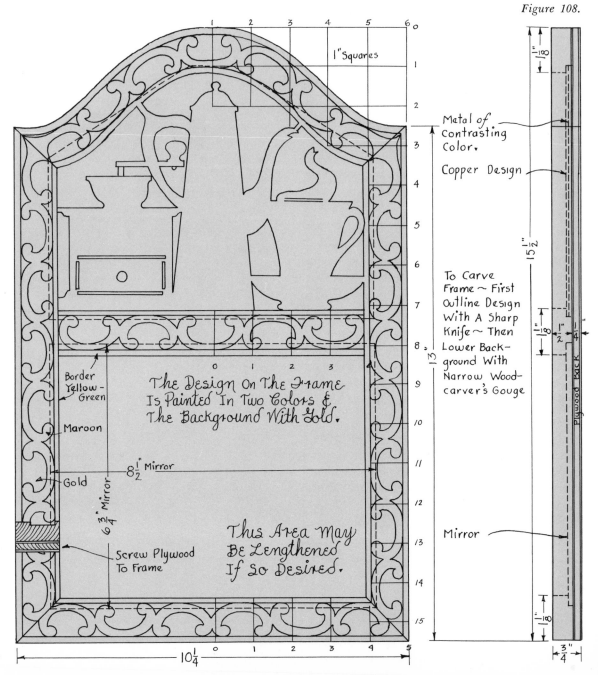

Figure 108.

1" Squares

Metal of
Contrasting
Color.

Copper Design

To Carve
Frame ~ First
Outline Design
With A Sharp
Knife ~ Then
Lower Back-
ground With
Narrow Wood-
carver's Gouge

Border
Yellow-
Green

Maroon

Gold

The Design On The Frame
Is Painted In Two Colors &
The Background With Gold.

8½" Mirror

6¾" Mirror

Screw Plywood
To Frame

This Area May
Be Lengthened
If So Desired.

Mirror

Plywood Back

15½"

13

1⅛"

1"
2

1"
4

1⅛"

1⅛"

Figure 107.   10¼   ¾"

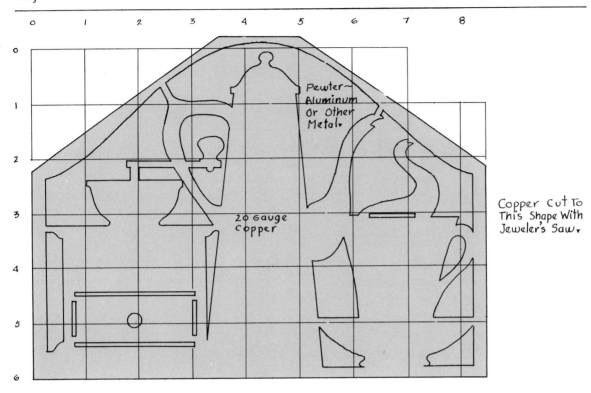

Figure 109.

Project 12

Looking Glass with Comb Tray

This looking glass is a useful project with a very interesting carving design. A kitchen or hallway would be a good place to hang it. The dovetailing, shown in Figure 113 in detail, is another nice feature. For more information about dovetailing, see Project 5, the carved box with the bird design.

This looking glass is shown partly assembled in Chapter 2, with the design transferred to the wood, ready to carve. The frame holding the mirror can be made and glued together before the stiles and top rail are carved. Notice that the background is neither smooth nor level but lowered just enough around the design so the design can be raised sufficiently to model the leaves, birds, flowers, and so on. The background surface is then carefully modeled with gouge cuts going in one direction. The surface texture thus achieved throws the design into sharp relief.

Figure 112 shows a good way to fasten the mirror to the frame. Two flat corner metal mending plates were sawed in half to make the four needed to hold the mirror and plywood in place.

The frame is made of cherry wood.

Figure 110. Looking glass with comb tray.

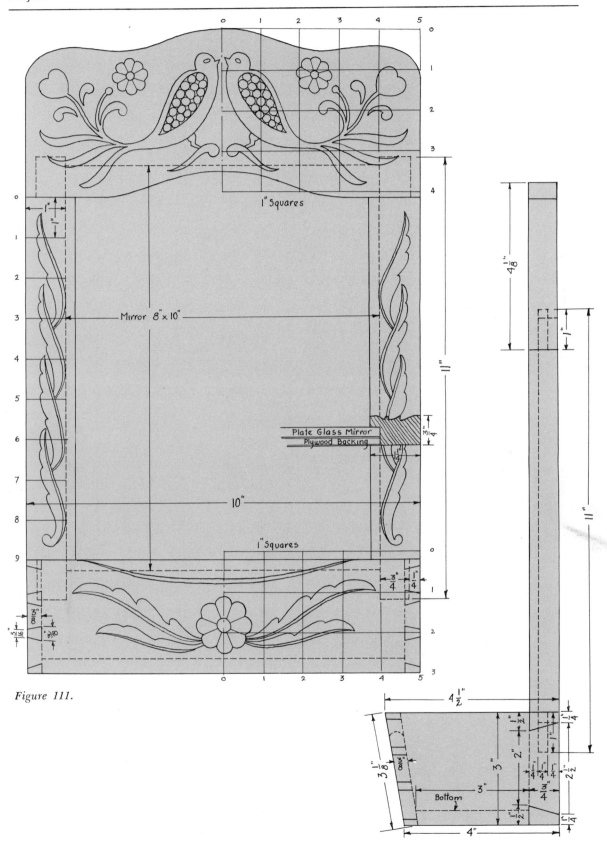

Figure 111.

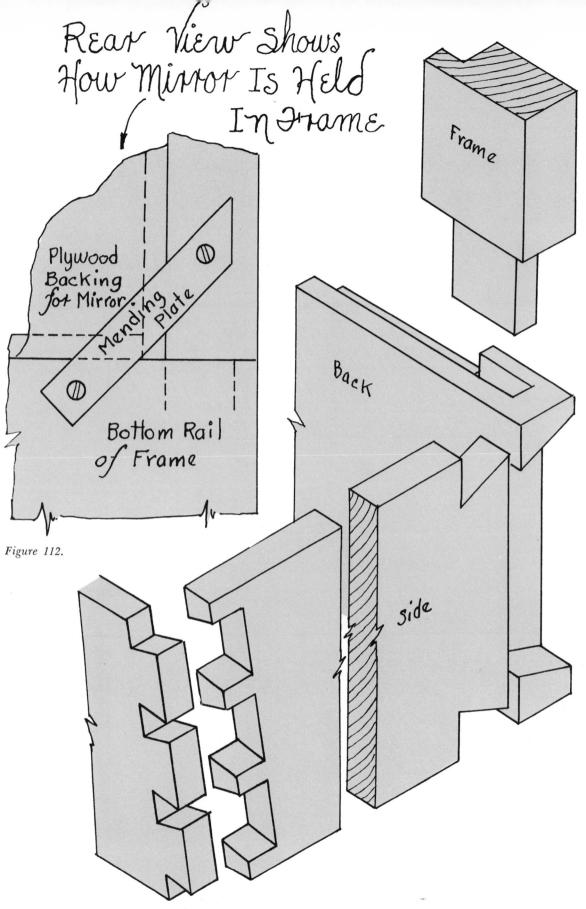

Rear View Shows
How Mirror Is Held
In Frame

Frame

Plywood
Backing
for Mirror.

Mending Plate

Bottom Rail
of Frame

Figure 112.

Back

side

Figure 113.

with dark gold bronze paint, then varnished with several coats, and the final coat was rubbed down with pumice and oil.

Project 13
Candlestick

Projects turned on the wood lathe are often well suited for wood-carving decoration. This black walnut candlestick consists of three parts, all turned on the lathe: the base, the shaft, and the cup-shaped holder.

The base of the stand is turned on a faceplate. A hole is drilled partway through it to hold the shaft. The shaft may be carved while still mounted between the lathe centers.

The cup should be turned separately, since this makes it easier to hollow the inside. Turn a cylinder on the lathe, 3¼″ in diameter and 1″ or so longer than the 3¼″ needed. Screw the bottom end to a faceplate, and hollow the inside first. Then turn the outside. Drill the hole in the bottom, and then saw off the remaining waste. In this photo the cup of the candlestick was carved while mounted between the lathe centers. By doing it this way, it is easy to rotate the project and get at all sides to do the work. If the lathe has an index head that makes it possible to lock the work into any position of the 360-degree circumference, this way of holding it for carving can hardly be improved upon.

I suggest that the rim around the top of the cup be turned a little larger than shown here and be curved upward a little on top.

Burnt umber stain was used for this project. The area surrounding the leaves was painted

Figure 114. This black walnut candlestick consists of three parts, all turned on the lathe.

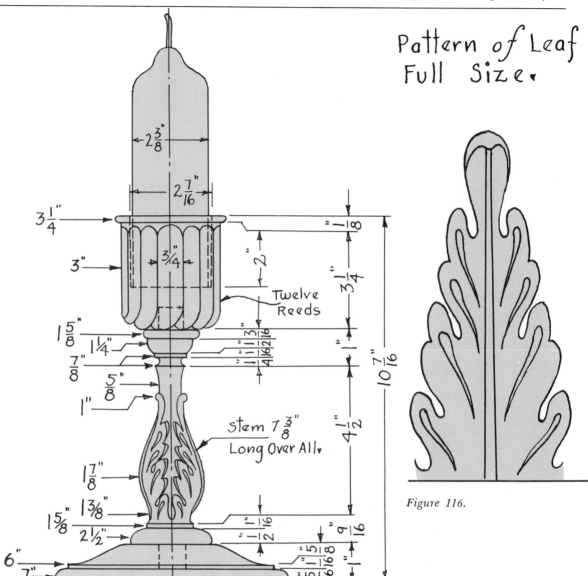

Pattern of Leaf
Full Size.

2 3/8"

2 7/16"

3 1/4"

3"

3/4"

Twelve
Reeds

2"

3 1/4"

1 5/8"   1 1/4"

7/8"

5/8"

1"

Stem 7 3/8"
Long Over All.

1 7/8"

1 5/8"   1 3/8"

2 1/2"

10 7/16"

4 1/2"

6"

7"

Figure 115.

Figure 116.

Project 14
Dolphin Candlestick

A dolphin candlestick like the one in Figure 117 would be a handsome addition to any table setting. A pair would be even better, and the time spent in carving them would be well repaid. Hard mahogany or walnut would be most suitable.

The base and the holder for the candle could be square instead of turned. Figure 119 illustrates the holder turned, and in Figure 120 you can see how to drill the hole for the candle before the outside is turned. Drilling the hole first minimizes the danger of splitting this piece after having carved it, and the wood can be mounted in the lathe by fitting a dowel into the hole.

Cross-section views at A-B and C-D show that the body is rounded before carving is started. If the head is to be fitted to the base as shown here, this should be done before carving on the other parts is started. By flattening the spot where the head and base meet, the fitting may be simplified. Scales on the dolphin may be hollowed slightly, as shown in the sampler in Figure 28 in Chapter 2, or they may be left flat, as shown here.

Figure 117.

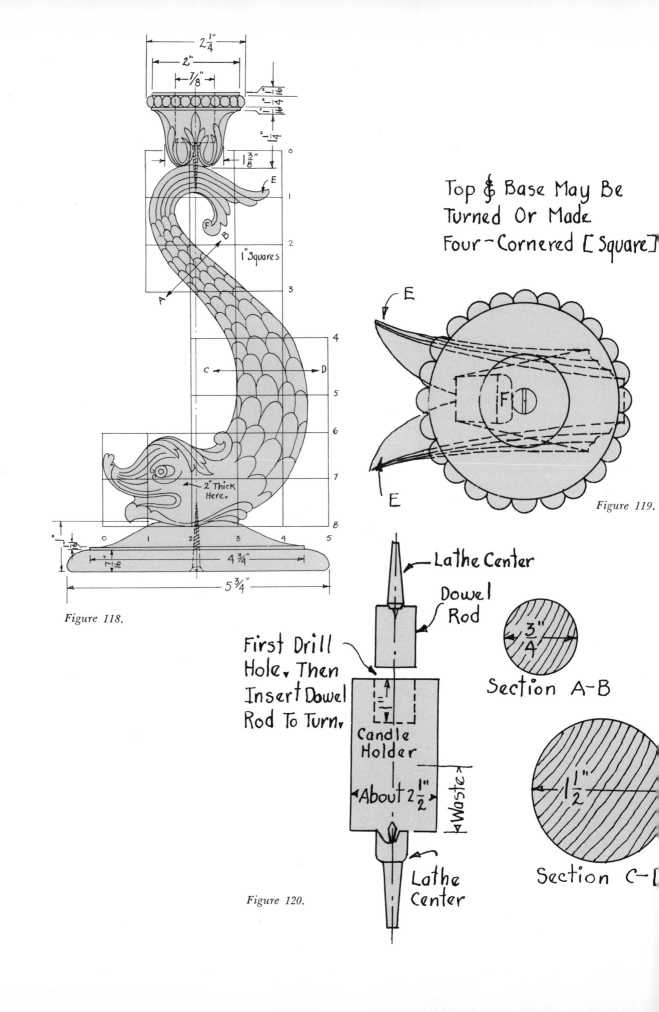

2¼"

2"

⅞"

1/16"
1/16"
1/64"

¼"

1⅜"

O

E

1

2

B

1"Squares

3

A

4

C ←――→ D

5

6

7

2" Thick
Here

8

O   1   2   3   4   5

⅞/16"

7/16"

4¾"

5¾"

Figure 118.

Top & Base May Be
Turned Or Made
Four-Cornered [Square]

E

F

E

Figure 119.

Lathe Center

Dowel
Rod

First Drill
Hole. Then
Insert Dowel
Rod To Turn.

Candle
Holder

←About 2½"→

←Waste→

Lathe
Center

Figure 120.

¾"

Section A-B

1½"

Section C-D

Project 15

"Beauty Is Truth" Plaque

This wall plaque, a quotation from John Keats's "Ode on a Grecian Urn," is simple in design (Figure 121). Simple things often have greater charm than elaborate ones, but they are often more difficult to create.

Hand-carved lettering incised in wood or chiseled in stone is usually meant to catch the eye. The border and the simple ornament near the top add considerably to the flavor of this design.

Carving lettering in wood requires careful and precise cutting with sharp tools. This plaque was carved on a ½" by 14¼" by 14¼" board of yellow poplar wood. The layout is shown in Figure 122. Once the design has been drawn on a smoothly sanded board, most of the lettering can be done with a short-bent V-tool. A ¼" straight chisel and a skew-bladed knife are useful for truing up the lettering. Chisels and knives may be used to do the butterfly-shaped ornament.

Figure 121. "Beauty Is Truth" plaque requires careful and precise lettering with sharp tools.

Figure 122.

Project 16
Leaf Plaque

In Chapter 2 I described some of the techniques used in carving this rather bold, eye-catching leaf plaque (Figure 123). Carved on a quarter-sawed white oak board and framed with molding made from plain-sawed boards, it illustrates the pattern differences resulting from these two methods of sawing lumber.

The bold design of the leaf blends well with the coarse texture of oak wood. The design could be used to make panels for a chest or a door in a house. In my house it graces a wall in the dining room—an interesting variation for a wall decoration.

The background area surrounding the leaf is painted with gold bronze paint, which does not completely hide the grain of the wood. Border areas and frame are stained with a transparent coat of burnt umber thinned with turpentine. The slightly lowered inside border of the frame molding is colored with yellow-green bronze paint. Over the leaf, which is stained like the surrounding border area, yellow, green, and orange colors are daubed on with an artist's brush and blended with the fingers. A pattern for this leaf can be made from Figure 124.

I was lucky enough to find a frame to fit the carving in a supermarket—they were being sold to frame pictures being given away in a sales promotion. An inexpensive frame like this can be found ready-made but would not be too difficult to make in a home workshop equipped with a table saw and wood-carving tools.

Figure 123. The bold design of the leaf blends well with the coarse texture of the wood.

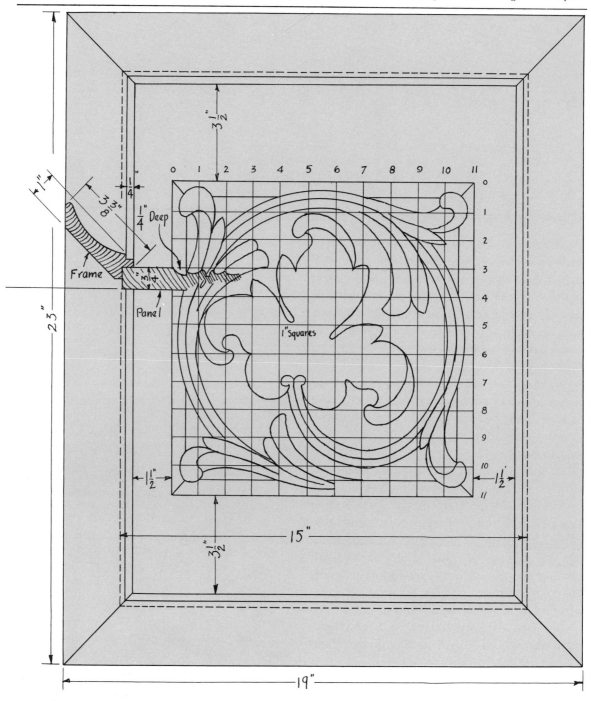

Figure 124.

Project 17

Wall Plaque with Pennsylvania Dutch Fractur *Motif*

Figure 125 shows an interesting wall plaque. The motif is adapted from a *fractur* painting I designed years ago.

The carving on this plaque can be done in much the same manner as on the box in Project 5 with the carved bird on its lid. The border of the plaque could be a separate frame, carved like the picture frame on the painting of the village blacksmith. It is shown here as an integral part of the carving itself.

A frame around such a wide board might help to keep it from warping; I suggest using poplar wood. The danger of warping can be minimized if a board of this width is first sawed into several pieces and then reglued. Even if the pieces are glued back exactly as they were before, this reduces the grain pull that tends to warp a board. And if alternate pieces are turned over, end for end, these strains will be reduced even more.

The lettering need not be drawn on the board until all the background has been lowered and the rest of the carving completed and cleaned up. Color work, like the kind described for the leaf plaque, will accentuate the beauty of the carving. Such color work is especially appropriate here, because Pennsylvania Dutch *fractur* art was lavishly colored, often with unorthodox color combinations.

Figure 125.

Project 18
Spread Eagle

The great bald eagle, clutching draped American flags and a star-studded shield, has a 4-foot wing spread (Figure 126).

The wood is California sugar pine and the layout for the carving can be taken from the working drawings, Figures 128 and 129. The lower plank is 1¼″ thick, glued to a width of 22″, and 48″ long. This is marked Section 1 on the drawing. The shield is superimposed over this with glue; this is Section 2. It is a piece of wood ⅞″ thick, 10″ wide, and 10″ long. Section 4, from which most of the head is carved, can have the same diameter at its base as Section 3, but the size varies a bit on the drawing to make it easier to distinguish one from the other. Section 5 consists of two ⅝″ blocks glued to the top of the shield to carve the feet. Two small blocks of wood ¾″ thick are glued to the flat for the tassels. An examination of the partly finished carving shown in Figure 127 will help make all this easier to understand.

When the planks have been glued, most of the outline shaping can be done on a band saw. However if your band saw is only a 12″ one, some of the waste between the wings and the flagpoles may have to be removed with a keyhole saw because there will not be enough room to maneuver some of the turns on a small band saw.

Enlarging the pattern to its actual size will take some time and patience. With this in mind I have eliminated as much detailing on the right wing as possible. Graph square lines are numbered to make it easy to locate areas. Around

the head this simplification was not entirely possible; but there slight variations of feather arrangement will not matter too much. Attention to detail in the wing feathers, however, can make quite a bit of difference in this imposing carving.

Care should also be taken to get the colors of the flag as close to the original as possible, and some careful brush work is required to do the stars and the areas around them. The burnt umber stain for the wings I made quite dark, and, wishing to give the carving a slightly antique look, I stained the striped area of the flags with the burnt umber stain before painting over it. Single coats of red and white enamel over the stain gave just about the right effect. I also did the same thing on the eagle's neck feathers.

Figure 126. This carving of the great bald eagle has a 4-foot wing spread.

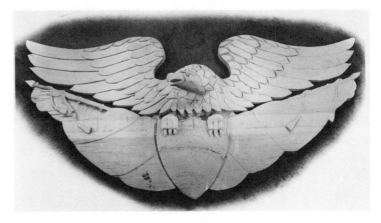

Figure 127. Spread eagle, partly finished, shows how the pieces are fitted together.

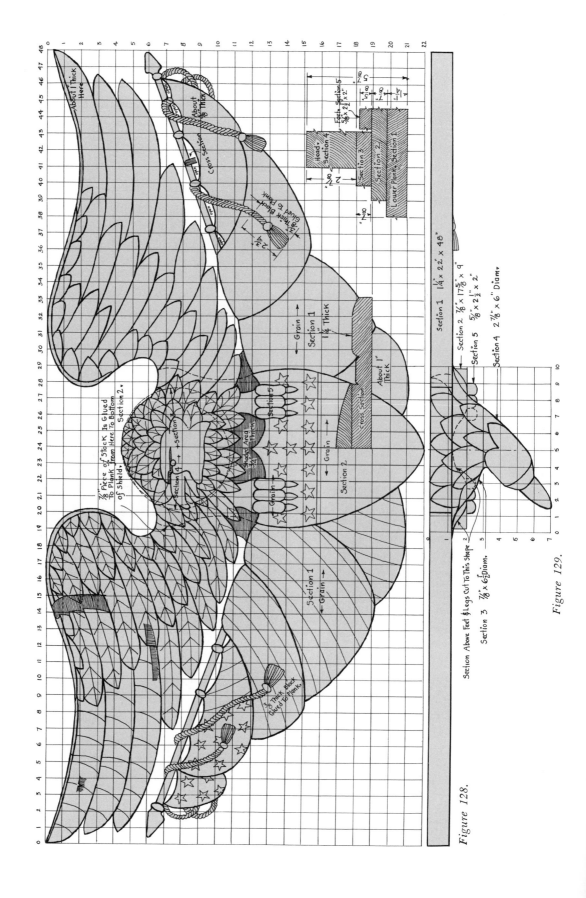

About 1" Thick Here

About 1/8" Thick

Cross Section

1/8" Thick Block Glued To Plank

2 3/4"

Grain →

Section 1
1/4" Thick

Section 2

About 1" Thick

Cross Section

← Grain

Section 2

Grain →

Grain →

Shaded Area 1/4" Thick

Section 4 →

← Section 5

Section 5

Section 2 ▾

1/8" Piece of Stock Is Glued To Plank from Here To Bottom of Shield.

Section 1
← Grain

3/8" Thick Block Glued To Plank

Head-
Section 4

Section 3

Section 2

Each Section 5
5/8 x 2 1/4 x 2"

Lower Plank, Section 1

Figure 128.

Section Above Feet & Legs Cut To This Shape

Section 3   7/8 x 6 1/2 Diam.

Section 1   1 1/4" x 22" x 48"

Section 2   7/8" x 17 5/8" x 9"

Section 5   5/8" x 2 1/2" x 2"

Section 4   2 7/8" x 6" Diam.

Figure 129.

Chapter 2 shows some of this carving being done.

To smooth the inside of the bowl properly, use curved scrapers after the chiseling is nearly completed. Careful sanding finishes the job.

Project 19
Carved Fruit Bowl

The small carved fruit bowl shown in Figure 130 serves as an introduction to the three-dimensional carving of the kind that has to be done with animals or human figures. This bowl, made of walnut, is a form of wood sculpture. Details for making it are found in Figure 132.

Figure 131 shows how work on the bowl is begun. First, draw the shape of the top on the block, and then saw the outside to shape on the band saw. The inside of the bowl is then chopped out with a large carpenter's gouge. When this is done, draw the pattern of the scallops (the undulations where the ribs are carved in the side of the bowl end) for the bottom of the bowl on the lower side of the block. With the band saw table tilted to an angle of about 30 degrees, saw off the scallops on the lower two-thirds of the bowl all around. While doing this be careful to keep the band saw blade about ½" away from the scallops on top of the bowl, to keep enough wood to carve the scallops vertically when carving the outside of the bowl.

After sawing the outside to this angle all around, trim the saw cuts with chisels and a rasp to make the sides smooth enough to redraw the lines for carving the scallops and fillets (the narrow flat sections between the convex and the hollowed-out ribs on each side of the bowl).

Carve the beads and carefully smooth the protruding, or convex, ribs between the coves. Then draw the coves (the hollowed, or concave, areas on all sides), leaving a fillet between each bead and cove, and then carve them. Figure 40 in

Figure 130. The carved fruit bowl is an introduction to three-dimensional carving.

Figure 131. Roughing out the carved fruit bowl which has been sawed to shape on a band saw.

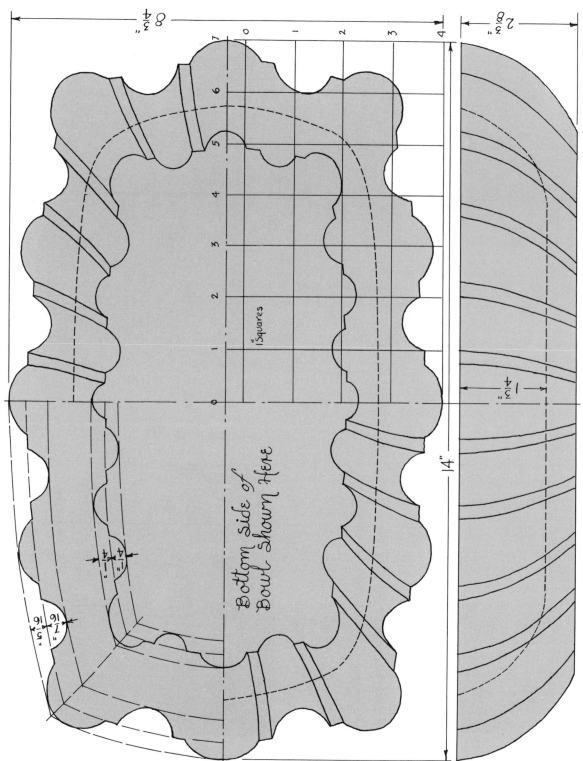

Figure 132.

Project 20
Sculptured Inkwell and Pen and Pencil Tray

The pen and pencil tray shown in Figure 133 dresses up a desk, and the inkwell holds a 2-ounce bottle of ink, as shown in Figure 136. The top of the well is hollowed out in such a way that the ink bottle can be lifted out and replaced. Once the well has been made to fit a particular bottle, it is a good idea to save it; should bottle sizes change it can then be refilled from one that may not fit.

The wood used to make this project is California sugar pine. The small carved horse can be exchanged for a carved dog, or any other animal you prefer.

Figure 134 shows that a thinner piece of wood for the front of the tray was glued to the heavier block in back. This makes it easier to shape this part, because the pen and pencil trough can be hollowed out before gluing the two pieces together.

Carving on the base of the project is easily done with gouges, and sharp corners should be softened all around. The upper part of the inkwell is glued to the base. Two pieces of wood can be hollowed out with gouges and then glued together to form the well for the ink bottle. Then the design can be drawn on the outside and the inkwell can be carved.

Another method for cutting the hole is to use a hole saw on the drill press. In Figure 134 the hole saw is being used to cut the hole partway into the base. The blade shown in this illus-tration is not wide enough to cut halfway through the carved upper section, and for this reason I made the upper section in two parts as described above and hollowed the inside with gouges and files. However, wider hole-cutting saw blades are made and could be used to saw out the hole using a piece of wood thick enough, or from a glued piece. The hole should be cut before any carving is done so that the clamps used to hold the block while the hole is being bored will not damage the carving.

If the block is clamped in a hand screw, and the hand screw is clamped to the drill press table, there is little likelihood that you will split the block when sawing out the hole. The drill that centers the saw must be started in the exact center of the block so the holes will align properly when they meet. Figure 135 shows how the corners of the inkwell at the top of the hole must be gouged out to make room for removing the bottle.

A pattern for the leaves on the side of the well can be made from Figure 140. They are not very large, and the modeling is finely detailed, so it is well worth taking the time to shape them carefully. The lid is easy to make and carve.

The small horse is carved from a block of sugar pine 1¼" thick, 4½" wide, and 4" high. Notice that the wood grain runs vertically. The tail is carved separately and glued on as shown in Figure 139.

Saw the blank to size, then draw the side view of the horse on it. Band saw this to shape. The waste between the legs at the back and front can best be sawed out by hand with a coping saw. Once sawed to shape, most of the carving can be done with a pocketknife, though it is better to use a small gouge to shape the belly at the top of the legs. A gouge is also used to shape the inside of the ears. Hair on the mane is carved with a short-bent V-tool, as is the tail. Numbers at various locations on the sketches indicate thickness in sixteenths of an inch at each such place.

The upper part of the well and the horse are glued to the base after they have been carved. A brass knob is screwed to the top of the lid.

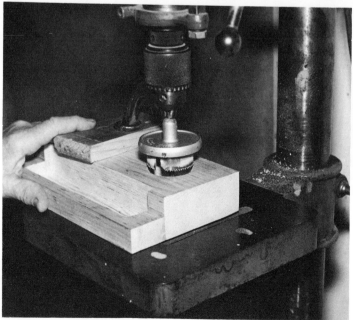

Figure 133. Sculptured inkwell, pen and pencil tray.

Figure 134. Hole saw is convenient tool to cut hole partway into the base.

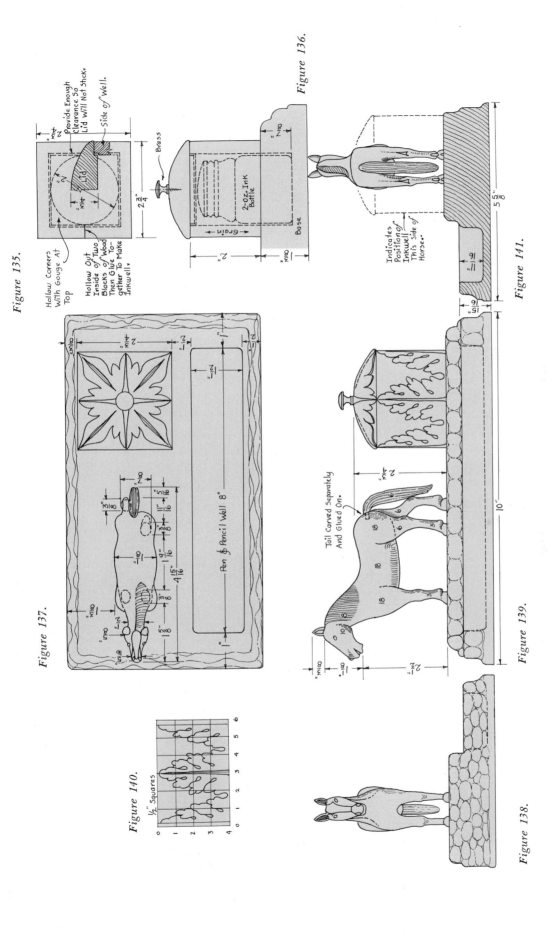

Figure 135.

Provide Enough Clearance So Lid Will Not Stick.

Side of Well.

Hollow Corners With Gouge At Top

Lid

$2\frac{2}{4}$"

$2\frac{2}{4}$"

Hollow Out Inside of Two Blocks of Wood Then Glue To-gether To Make Inkwall.

Figure 136.

Brass

2"

2-Oz. Ink Bottle

Grain

Base

Figure 141.

Indicates Position of Inkwell This Side of Horse.

$5\frac{5}{8}$"

$\frac{11}{16}$"

Figure 137.

$2\frac{3}{4}$"

$\frac{1}{2}$"

$1\frac{1}{2}$"

$\frac{3}{8}$"

$\frac{5}{16}$"

$\frac{11}{16}$"

$\frac{3}{8}$"

$\frac{9}{16}$"

$4\frac{15}{16}$"

$\frac{3}{8}$"

$\frac{5}{8}$"

$\frac{9}{16}$"

Pen & Pencil Well 8"

1"

Figure 140.

½" Squares

Tail Carved Separately And Glued On.

$2\frac{3}{4}$"

10"

$2\frac{1}{2}$"

$\frac{15}{16}$"

Figure 139.

Figure 138.

Project 21

Horse

The only difference you'll find between the horse shown in Figure 133 and the one shown here is the size.

The pattern for this horse can be made from the drawing in Figure 148. On this drawing you will also find the numbers indicating thicknesses. See the instructions for the inkwell horse for carving directions; the wood is California sugar pine.

Glass beads for eyes were glued into drilled sockets in the head.

Figure 142.

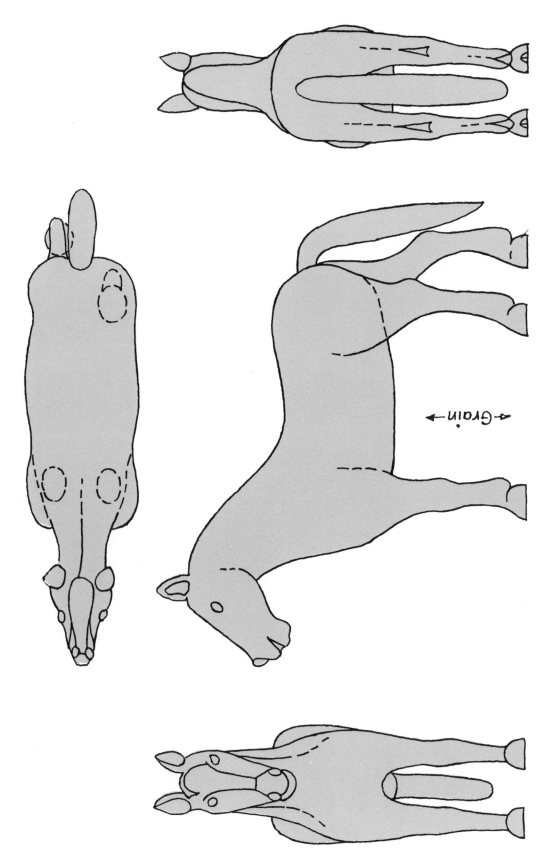

Grain

Figure 143.

Figure 144.
Figure 146.

Figure 145.
Figure 147.

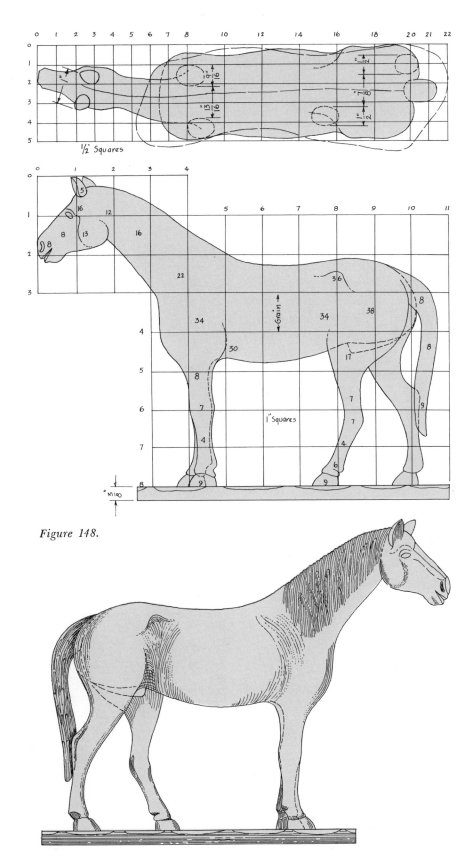

Figure 148.

Figure 149.

Project 22
Camel

were photographed. Some were varnished, and several, like the bison and the bear, had been stained. The last coat of varnish should always be a satin finish to take off the objectionable shiny appearance left by the high-gloss varnish.

The process of carving four-footed animals is much the same for most animal figures. After the kind of wood and the thickness of the block have been determined, a side view of the animal is drawn on a piece of paper, and from this pattern the outline is transferred to the wood. Also locate where the feet will be on the bottom of the block. The block is then sawed to its approximate shape. The waste areas between the legs and the ears are then removed, usually with a coping saw. This leaves the actual shape of the animal well established. After rounding sharp corners, edges, and lines and doing some modeling on legs, ears, and face, you have reached the stage where a few minor details—lines to simulate hair or fur, cutting eyes and nostril holes—complete the task. This may seem like an oversimplification, but many beginners are astonished at how easy they find it to carve a variety of animals once they have done one. Numbers at various locations on the sketches indicate thickness in sixteenths of an inch at each such place.

These animal carvings, though quite large in size, were mostly done with knives and carved out of California sugar pine. Carving chisels and sometimes wood rasps were also used in certain areas, such as under the camel's belly where legs and body are joined.

Some animals in this collection are glued to a base, giving the carved figure greater stability and preventing slender legs from being broken.

Most of the animals had no finish when they

Figure 150.

Figure 151.

Figure 152.
Figure 153.

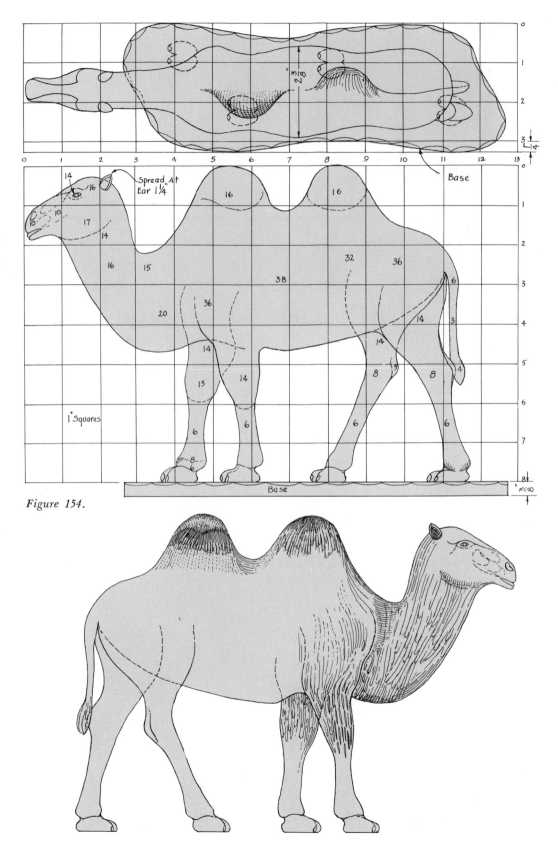

Figure 154.

Figure 155.

Project 23
The Bison

Figures 156 to 159 show every side of this impressive animal carving. Figure 26 in Chapter 2 shows the blank sawed to shape. This was done on a band saw, and a center line was then drawn around the block with a soft pencil. The blank for this carving was 3⅜″ thick.

Drill holes through the blank at the back to separate the tail from the body. It is best to drill these halfway through from both sides so the wood will not splinter when the drill comes through on the other side. Also drill holes into both sides of the head for the horns.

Figure 157 shows some of the carving started, and the tail and left hind leg almost finished. Some of the rough shaping on the head, neck, and body has been done with gouges. A lot of this boasting-in, or rough cutting and shaping, may be done by fastening the blank in a vise, or even by fastening it to the top of a workbench with a C-clamp, and then shaping it with a mallet and gouges.

Be careful when carving the legs of the bison, or any other animal, first to locate where the feet will go on the bottom of the block of wood, because the amount of spread where the feet are located seldom is as great as the widest parts of the body of the animal.

In addition to locating the position of the feet on the bottom of the block, you should then draw the legs on both sides of the block as carefully as possible with a felt marker or soft pencil. You are then ready to saw out parts of the waste.

In doing this, however, keep in mind that the two hind legs of the bison are not directly across from each other, which is why the photo of the blank appears to have three legs on each side. Most of the wood not required for the legs will be cut off from the side where it is not needed before final shaping and modeling of the leg takes place.

The waste between the legs on the inside may be sawed out with a coping saw, by hand, rather than doing it on a jigsaw, a band saw, or any power-driven saw. With proper care it is possible to drill holes on a drill press or with an electric hand drill to remove some waste parts, or to make way for inserting the coping saw blade, but you must be careful not to drill too close to the finish lines of the carving when doing this.

Once as much waste as possible has been removed, either by sawing or drilling, rough modeling can be started—thinning parts of the body and starting to give it some shape. I prefer to rough out all sides of a figure before paying too much attention to the finer detail work, but sometimes there are exceptions. Numbers at various locations on the sketches indicate thickness in sixteenths of an inch at each such place.

Once the roughing-in has been done on a carving of this kind, most of the subsequent modeling can be done with knives. This way, the block of wood can be held in one hand while the other hand does the carving and shaping. It is easy to move the work constantly from one

Figure 156.

position to another, readily accommodating the tool to changes in the grain. Hair lines shown over the front of the body are cut in with a V-tool.

Eyes on this animal are not difficult to carve. Outline the eyeball with the point of a sharp penknife, or the pointed end of a skew blade, and then shape the ball by slicing off thin chips of wood all around the edges.

The tiny ears are hardly noticeable—little more than imperceptible bulges covered with hair.

Saw out two horns on a jigsaw, and round them with a knife. After they have been sanded, glue them into the holes that have been drilled into both sides of the head.

After all the shaping has been done, but before cutting lines to simulate hair, sandpaper all parts of the carving. Do the final sanding with 6/0 garnet paper. Then cut hair lines with a narrow V-tool.

The finish on the bison is walnut stain, which is quite dark, followed with coats of varnish. Each coat should be rubbed with steel wool and cleaned thoroughly before the next one is put on. The final coat should be satin varnish, and this may be polished with wax when thoroughly dry.

Figure 157. Roughly cut and shaped bison. This stage can be reached very quickly, even by a beginner.

Figure 158.

Figure 159.

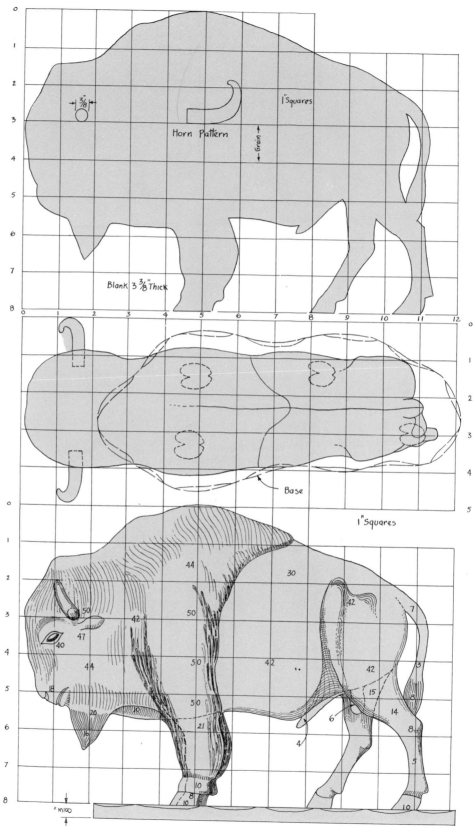

Figure 160.

Figure 161.

Figure 162.

Project 24

Cow

I once read that an artist supposedly said, "The cow is a most unfortunate creature from an artistic standpoint, because she's unshapely, poorly proportioned, and therefore makes a poor model for the artist." I hope this reproduction will persuade many wood-carvers to disagree with him. In my opinion Figures 163 to 166 show the cow to be well worth carving.

Figure 167 is a three-view drawing from which full-size patterns can be made. Numbers at various locations on the sketches indicate thickness in sixteenths of an inch at each such place.

Holes are drilled into both sides of her head for the horns, which are carved and then glued. This makes shaping the head and ears much easier.

Like all the other animals in this collection, the cow is carved from California sugar pine, and the grain of the wood runs vertically. A block of wood measuring 3″ x 9½″ x 6¼″ is needed.

Figure 163.

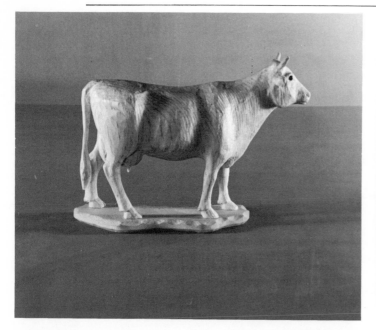

Figure 165.

Figure 164.

Figure 166.

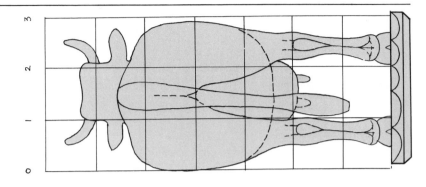

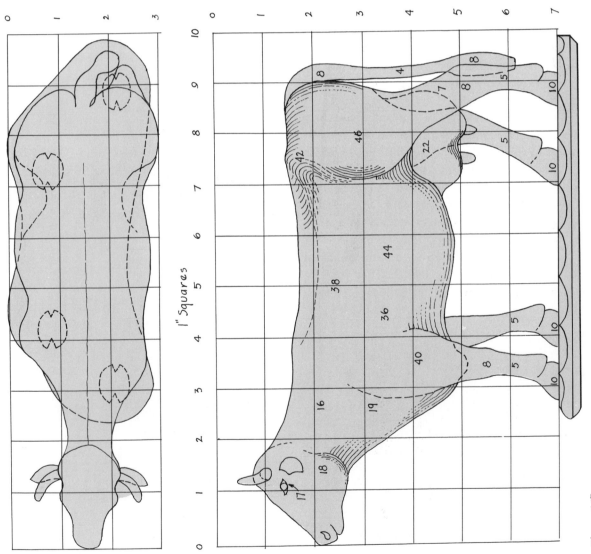

1" Squares

Figure 167.

Project 25
Elephant

There are carvings of elephants much more difficult to reproduce than this one, for instance an elephant up on his two hind legs, with trunk threateningly upraised and forelegs pawing the air. This mild-mannered elephant is relatively easy to carve and yet challenging enough to make the project interesting.

The patterns to cut him out and shape him are shown in Figure 171. After you saw the elephant to shape on a band saw, little more needs to be done except to round his body, head, trunk, and legs. Forming the ears and tail is perhaps the most difficult part of the work. The eyes are black beads glued into holes made with a drill. If you have never carved animals before, this elephant is a good one to start with. Numbers at various locations on the sketches indicate thickness in sixteenths of an inch at each such place.

Figure 168.

Figure 169.
Figure 170.

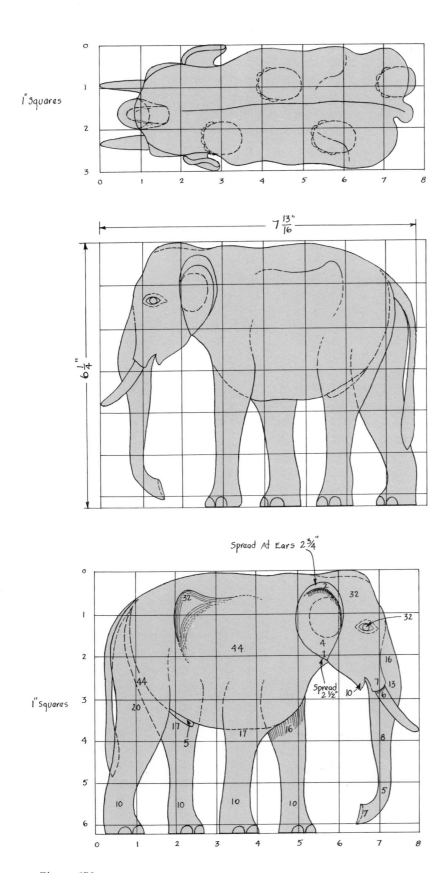

1" Squares

7 13/16"

6 1/4"

Spread At Ears 2 3/4"

1" Squares

Figure 171.

Project 26
Brahman Bull

Shaping the tail, head, legs, and body requires careful modeling to get the right effects. Study the photographs carefully and check the numbers on Figure 176 indicating thicknesses in sixteenths of an inch. Lines showing wrinkles in the skin around his neck are made with a small veiner. When completed, this carving should give you a real sense of accomplishment.

An animal that presents more of a challenge is the Brahman bull, shown in Figures 172 to 176. To carve him you will need a block of California sugar pine 3½″ thick, 13″ wide, and 7¼″ high. Again the grain of the wood must run vertically.

Stock as thick as this must sometimes be glued. The stock used for the one here was 3″ thick, and small pieces had to be glued to both sides to make him as thick as he is in the midsection. Two blocks 1¾″ thick glued together would do better if the 3½″ is not available in one piece.

Draw a full-size pattern, which you can get from the side view at the bottom of Figure 176, and cut the figure to this shape on a band saw. The horns are made separately and glued into holes drilled on both sides of his head, as shown in Figure 174. In Figure 174 we also show the ends of both ears glued on. As you can see, if the block originally was only 3″ thick, and the total spread from ear tip to ear tip is 4⅝″ as shown in Figure 174, then about ⅞″ must be added to each ear to get that width.

Figure 174 also gives you the size of the pieces of wood you will need to carve the horns. You can determine how to shape these by studying the way they appear in the rectangle drawn around the horns in Figure 176 and the one around the horn in Figure 174. Once the horns are properly shaped and fitted to the holes, all you have to do is tilt them to the proper angle, as indicated in Figure 176. This shows the front of the horn about 1″ back from the tip of the nose.

Figure 172.

Figure 173.

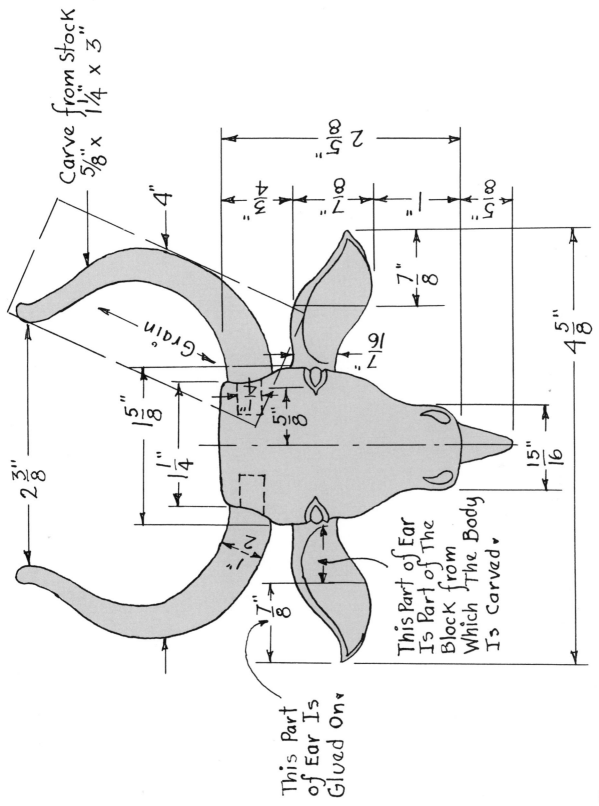

Figure 174.

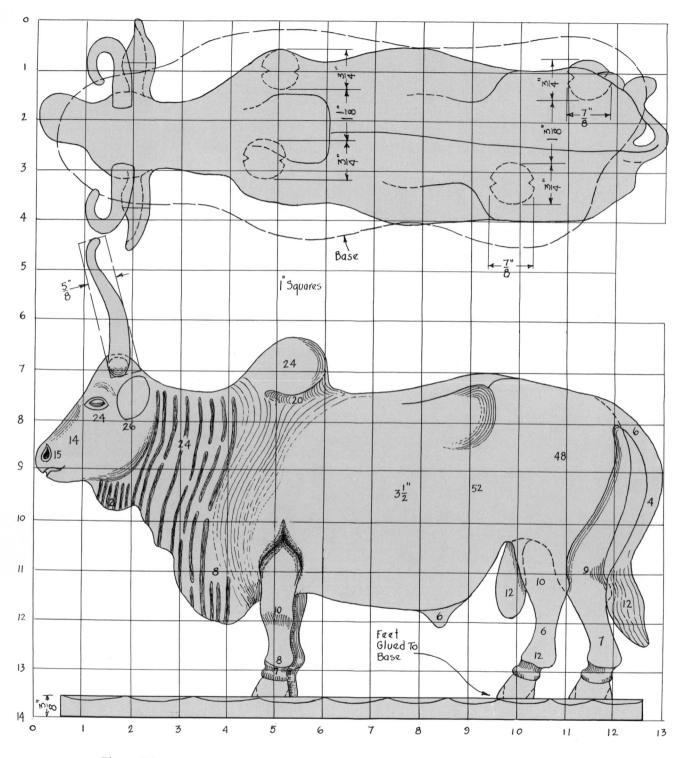

Figure 175.

Figure 176.

Project 27
Bear

This bear has just caught his noonday meal and is in an interesting pose for the carving. The rock he is standing on adds to the overall design.

As shown in Figure 181 he is carved from a single block of wood 3″ thick, 7¼″ wide, and 7⅝″ high. This being the case, it is necessary to drill holes under his body to take out most of the waste wood before shaping on the inside parts can be done. Numbers at various locations on the sketches indicate thickness in sixteenths of an inch at each such place.

Much of the carving can be done with knives, but it is much easier to use chisels for a large part of it. Modeling on the body is simple, with the exception of the face. The tiny marks simulating fur are made with a veining tool.

The bear was stained a dark brown, achieved by thinning Vandyke brown color in oil with turpentine. This is a darker brown than stain made with burnt umber. After you varnish him with a coat of glossy varnish, thinned with an equal amount of turpentine, a coat or two of satin finish varnish will give the right effect.

The fish may be colored using green, yellow, and gray and blending them to get the proper effect. The bear's rocky perch can also be colored, using gray, brown, and some blue, but thin these enough so the grain of the wood shows through. Watercolors are best for the fish and the rocks.

Figure 177.

Figure 178.

Figure 179.

Figure 180.

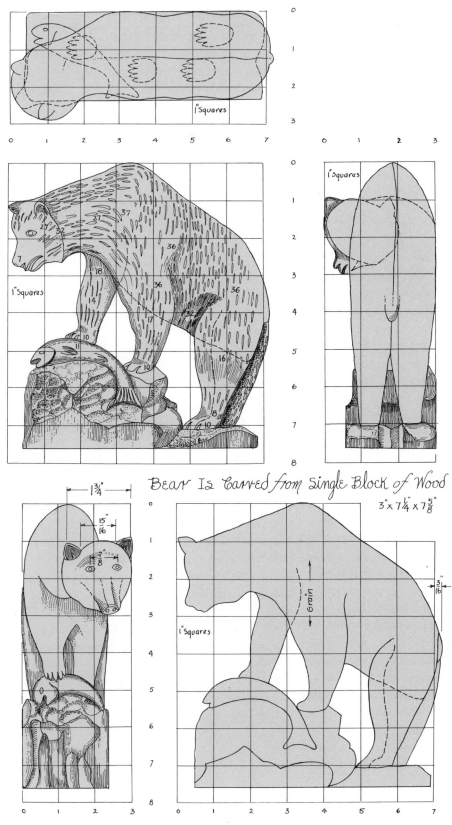

1" squares

1" Squares

1" squares

1" Squares

Bear Is Carved from Single Block of Wood

$3'' \times 7\frac{1}{4}'' \times 7\frac{5}{8}''$

$1\frac{3}{4}''$

$\frac{15}{16}''$

Grain

$\frac{3}{16}''$

Figure 181.

Project 28

Mama and Baby Hippopotamus

The hippopotamus may not be noted for outstanding beauty in the animal world, but this grouping has a special charm.

The carving is made in three parts, consisting of a mama, baby, and the base to which they are glued after they have been carved. The wood is California sugar pine, and on the animals the grain of the wood runs vertically. The drawings provide dimensions and body thicknesses to give additional help when you work on this appealing group.

Making the base requires no special skill or know-how as long as the size is right. Since the smaller animal is easier to carve, I advise doing it first. Saw the block to shape on a band saw, a jigsaw, or with a coping saw. This figure is easily held in one hand while it is being whittled to shape with a sharp knife. Begin carving by first rounding the back. The view from the front will help you to give it the proper shape.

Locate the eyes, ears, and nostril holes, and draw them with a soft lead pencil. Then carve the top of the head to shape. The ears on the small figure do not protrude as far as they do on the mama, but some care must still be taken to form them properly. A small gouge to shape the inside of the ear will help. The same is true for finishing off the nostril holes, which may be started by drilling shallow holes in the correct location, and then smoothing and shaping them with gouge and knife.

Roughly locate mouth and neck grooves; a gouge will also serve to shape these. The deep groove between the upper and lower lip may be cut with V-tool or with a pocketknife.

Once the blank has been sawed to shape and the waste between the two front legs and the two hind legs has been removed, rounding and forming the legs and belly present no great problem. Shaping the feet is not a hard job either since not much modeling is required.

The mama hippo is cut from a much larger piece, so you may find it easier to use chisels to carve her. You will also find the job can be made easier if at first you do not saw out the wood between the legs but leave it in place and screw to the waste part a block of wood large enough to clamp in a vise. This will allow you to use both hands while shaping the greater portion of the body and head.

While the modeling on the larger figure shows a little more detail than on the baby hippo, the procedure is much the same. The eyes and ears are larger and more carefully formed, and the tail is longer. When the head and upper section of the body have been carved, the waste between the legs may be sawed out, and the lower part of the body may be carved.

Finishing can consist of nothing more than waxing and polishing, as was done here; or the figures may be varnished after being rubbed down and polished with pumice stone and rubbing oil. They can be sprayed with lacquer, in which case the animals should be glued to the base before spraying takes place. It is possible to keep finish off the places where the feet are glued to the base by covering the points of contact with masking tape while applying finish to all other areas. If you do not wish to take this extra precaution, the feet of these animals are large enough to be screwed to the base from countersunk holes below.

Figure 182.

Figure 183.

Figure 184.

Figure 185.

Figure 186.

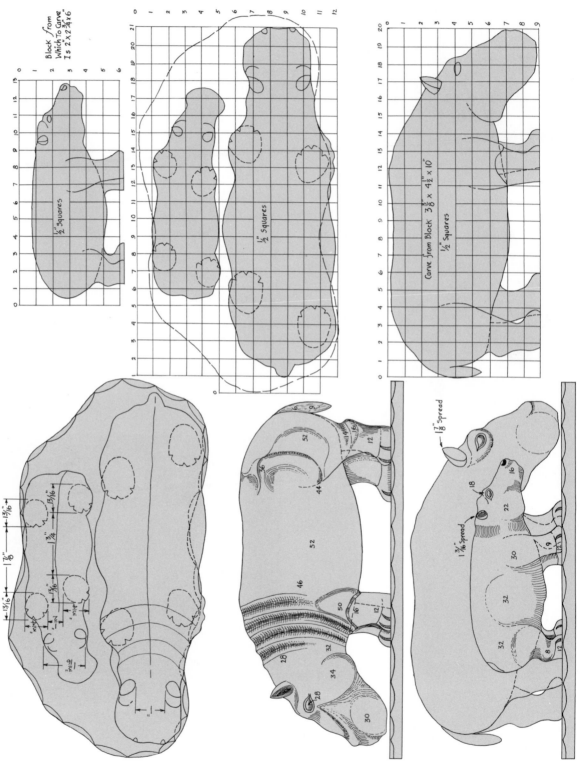

Figure 187.

Project 29
Bull Moose

The last of this interesting collection of carved animals is the bull moose. As you can see in Figure 191, the spread of his antlers makes him an impressive figure.

The pattern for the antlers is found in Figure 193. To carve them so that they have the proper contour requires a block of wood 1¼″ thick. The eight points on each antler will come to the upper surface of the block while the hollowing in the center makes the stem, where it enters his head, come to the base of the block.

Figure 193 gives the location of the holes into which the antlers are glued, in addition to other important details. Black beads may be glued into the eye sockets, as shown in the photographs, or the eyeballs may be carved as shown on the drawings. Numbers at various locations on the sketches indicate thickness in sixteenths of an inch at each such place.

When carved, the bull moose is a trim-looking creature despite his size, and a connoisseur of animal carvings would enjoy having one like this in his collection.

Figure 188.

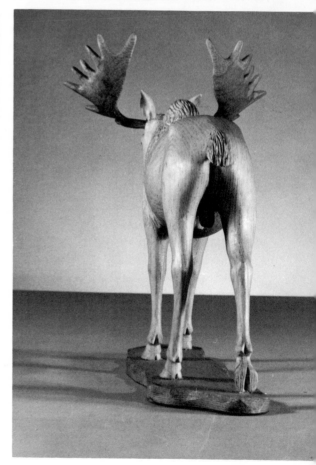

Figure 189.

Figure 190.

Figure 191.

Figure 192.

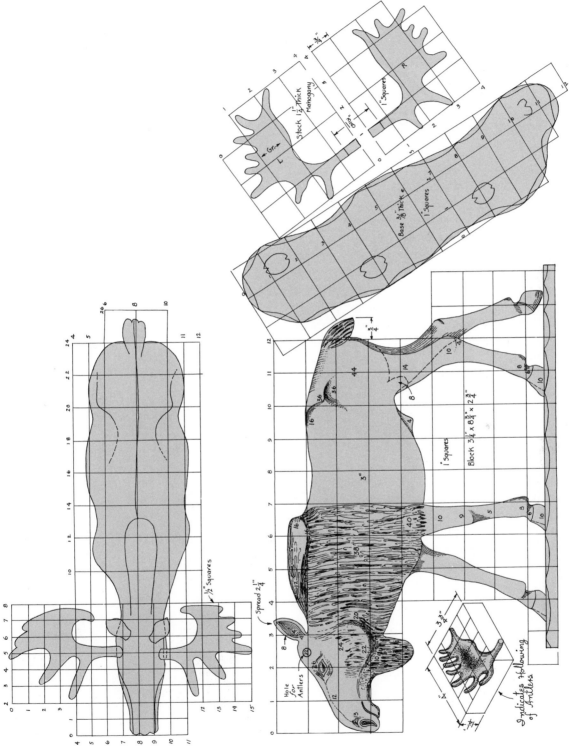

Figure 193.

Project 30
Eagle on a Perch

This regal bird has been reproduced in thousands of different ways by artists and craftsmen. The example shown here was carved of basswood and stained with burnt umber. The eagle was then mounted on a base painted flat black in front of a mirror, as shown in Figure 194, so that when viewed from almost any direction every beautiful detail of the carving can be seen and enjoyed.

The block of wood from which the eagle is carved should be 3″ thick, 7½″ wide, and 9″ high. It is best to use a piece of stock longer than 9″, however, so the bottom of the block can be fastened into a vise or some other holding device while carving it. A block 12″ or even 15″ long could be used, and the extra waste remaining at the bottom can be removed when the carving is completed.

When cutting out the blank, your first pattern will be the outline of the drawing showing the back of the eagle (Figure 202). Then to cut off the waste on the sides, make a pattern from the side view outline shown in Figure 200.

Start by shaping the tree trunk perch, and try to approximate the overall shape of the bird as accurately as you can, without actually doing the finer detailing on the feathers. This can wait until the head, wings, and body have their approximate shape. Wings thin out on their lower edges, but not so much that they become fragile, and tail feathers remain quite sturdy because

most of them are not separated from the eagle's perch.

Once the outline and general shaping have been accomplished, the finer details must be carved carefully. Feathers should be no great problem; draw them on the wood approximately as they are shown in Figures 199, 200, 201, and 202. Carving the head and feet may be a little more difficult.

Mirrors like the one we used to mount the carving may be found in shops that sell mirror glass and replace broken automobile glass. Notice in Figure 203 how the mirror is held in place with a few spots of epoxy glue at the top, by setting it into a rabbeted edge of the base, and then nailing the Masonite backing over it to the base block. After painting the base flat black, a long wood screw through it will hold the eagle in place.

Figure 194.

Figure 195.

Figure 197.

Figure 196.

Figure 198.

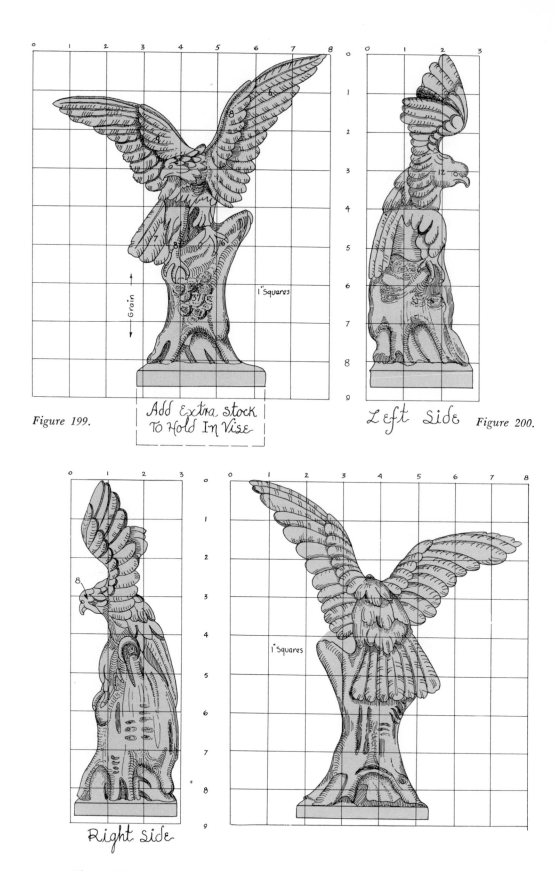

Figure 199.

Add Extra stock
To Hold In Vise

Left Side Figure 200.

Right side

Figure 201. Figure 202.

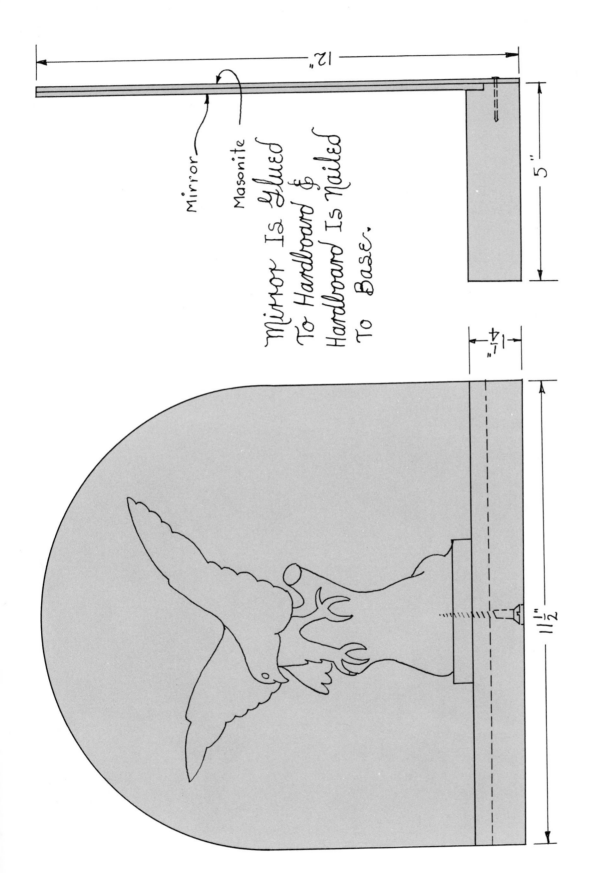

12"

Mirror

Masonite

Mirror Is Glued
To Hardboard &
Hardboard Is Nailed
To Base.

5"

1¼"

11½"

Figure 203.

Project 31
Christmas Elf

These elves were inspired by the Scandinavian folk tradition of Yule Nissen, or Christmas elf. The elf holding a lantern was the first version of this character. The only change made for the second was to dispose of the lantern, raise the right arm, and add the pipe. Possibilities for variations on this theme are endless. The wood used was white pine.

Figure 204.

Figure 205.

Figure 206.

Figure 207.

Figure 208.

Figure 209.

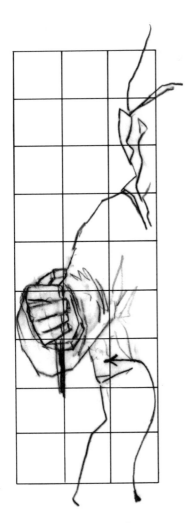

By Extending The
Arm Out He Holds
The Lantern.

Figure 210.

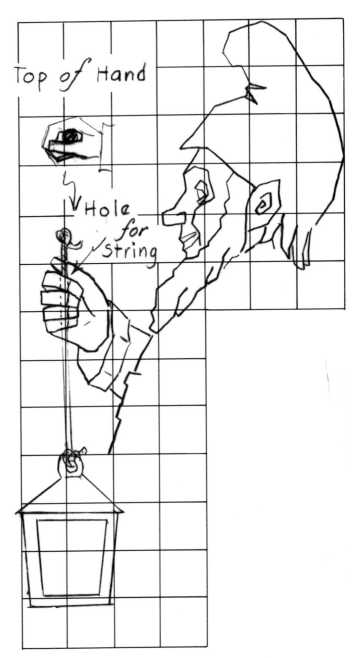

Top of Hand

Hole
for
string

Two Characters Can Be Made
From One By Changing The
Right Arm Position.

Figure 211.

Project 32
The Noble Red Man

do most of this work, unless the figure has been scaled down to a very small size.

After sawing the figure to approximately the right shape on the band saw, and after taking out the waste under the coat, I recommend using the photographs rather than the drawings as a guide. The drawings are helpful for placing details properly, but actual modeling can be better accomplished by studying the photographs.

The Indian in Figures 212 to 218 is definitely not a cigar store Indian, but rather the portrayal in wood of the red man and his nobility.

The carving was made from a glued block of kiln-dried mahogany measuring 7" by 8" by 28". Although a solid block of wood with these dimensions would be ideal for this carving, you can also glue it from kiln-dried stock 2" thick.

The Indian can be made smaller or larger by reducing or enlarging the scale of the graph shown in Figures 219 to 224. In these patterns each graph square represents 1" on the original carving; if the squares represent ½" instead of 1", then the carving could be made half the size of the original. For this a block measuring only 3½" by 4" by 14" would be needed. Further reductions in the scale of the graph squares will result in a carving which can be held in the hand and done with a pocketknife.

First make outline drawings of Figures 219 and 220. You can then saw the figure to this shape on the band saw. Much of the waste wood in spaces to be hollowed out, such as under his coat and between his legs, can be removed with an electric drill before starting to shape the legs, cape, and other major features. The lower parts of his body from the neck down, with the possible exception of the crook in his left arm where the modeling is a bit more complicated, should not prove too difficult for anyone who has had some experience carving in the round. The face and the bottom of the cape are a little more challenging. Carving chisels should be used to

Figure 212.

Figure 213.

Figure 214.

Figure 215.

Figure 216.

Figure 217.

Figure 218.

Figure 219.

Figure 220.

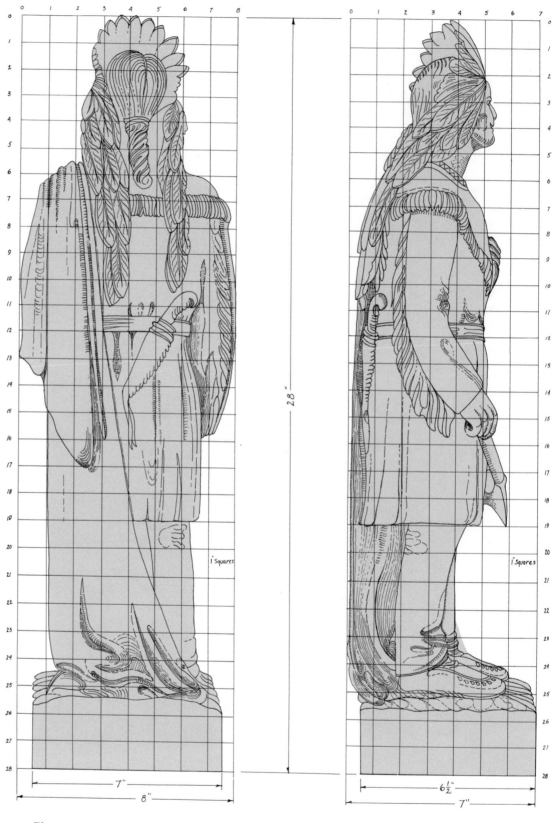

Figure 221.

Figure 222.

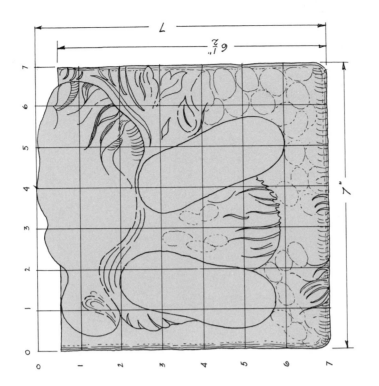

Figure 224.

1" Squares

Figure 223.

Index